Anywhere and Everywhere with Jesus

Karen Keaton

TEACH Services, Inc.
PUBLISHING
www.TEACHServices.com • (800) 367-1844

World rights reserved. This book or any portion thereof may not be copied or reproduced in any form or manner whatever, except as provided by law, without the written permission of the publisher, except by a reviewer who may quote brief passages in a review.

The author assumes full responsibility for the accuracy of all facts and quotations as cited in this book. The opinions expressed in this book are the author's personal views and interpretations, and do not necessarily reflect those of the publisher.

This book is provided with the understanding that the publisher is not engaged in giving spiritual, legal, medical, or other professional advice. If authoritative advice is needed, the reader should seek the counsel of a competent professional.

Copyright © 2018 Karen Keaton
Copyright © 2018 TEACH Services, Inc.
ISBN-13: 978-1-4796-0903-1 (Paperback)
ISBN-13: 978-1-4796-0904-8 (ePub)
Library of Congress Control Number: 2018935631

Table of Contents

Introduction v
Special Thanks vii
Chapter 1: Did You See My Angel? 9
Chapter 2: The Ten-Minute Limousine Ride. 11
Chapter 3: The Long Fall 13
Chapter 4: A Long, Rainy Night 15
Chapter 5: Surgery in North Carolina. 17
Chapter 6: The Lost Purse in Hawaii 19
Chapter 7: What Truk Did for Me!!! 21
Chapter 8: Rain, Rain Don't Go Away!!! 24
Chapter 9: A Truk Thanksgiving 26
Chapter 10: Windows of Heaven. 28
Chapter 11: No Knees on Sokez Rock 30
Chapter 12: Will I Ever Get Clean Again?. 32
Chapter 13: God's Perfect Timing 34
Chapter 14: Typhoons 36
Chapter 15: The Mute Second Grader 38
Chapter 16: Does God Have a Sense of Humor? 40
Chapter 17: The Long Way to Nowhere 42
Chapter 18: To Tell the Truth 44
Chapter 19: Angel in the Rice Paddy 46
Chapter 20: This Is Not Our Home. 48
Chapter 21: The Thanksgiving Bag 50

Chapter 22: Meet My Chinese Angel 52
Chapter 23: Jesus Love YOU!!! 54
Chapter 24: Chinese Mud Pit 56
Chapter 25: Monkeys on Emeishan. 58
Chapter 26: "Karen, It's Time to Get Up!" 60
Chapter 27: 2 A.M. Taxi Ride 63
Chapter 28: Follow Your Dreams 65
Chapter 29: The Lost Suitcase. 67
Chapter 30: Tears at the Airport 70
Chapter 31: A Break In-Between 72
Chapter 32: Resurrection 74
Chapter 33: Chinese Kindergarteners 76
Chapter 34: Way of Escape Already Planned 78
Chapter 35: Night with the Bad Girls 81
Chapter 36: Giardia 83
Chapter 37: Parrot Attack 85
Chapter 38: James 87
Chapter 39: An Alaskan Girl 89
Chapter 40: "Will That Not Be Awesome?" 91
Chapter 41: Why Pray?. 93
Chapter 42: Your Anywhere. 95
Conclusion. 97
Bible Studies 99
Answers 126

Introduction

The first line of my favorite Christian hymn is, *"Anywhere with Jesus, I can safely go," and* because this is the theme of my book, I hope and pray that as you read this part of my life story, you too, will realize you can go anywhere Jesus leads you. I believe that when the songwriter, Jessica B. Pounds, wrote this song, she truly meant **"anywhere."** As I reflect upon my past life, I can honestly say that there was never a time when I did not feel that Jesus was with me. So, my friend, it is my sincere desire that as you read the pages of this book, you too will reflect upon where you have been on your journey with Jesus and that you will praise HIM for leading you to where you are on this day in your life. Most of the experiences I will share with you, I was alone, or met people that I didn't know before, who journeyed with me for a while; but for the most part, it was just the LORD and me. There are two main reasons I wanted to share some of my experiences with you, and those are that I want you to look back over your own life and realize that no matter where you have been, you are never alone (whether in the physical or the spiritual sense, Jesus is always with you.) The second reason I wanted to share is to reach those of you who may be experiencing some downturn, and you feel that you are alone or that "anywhere" does not apply to you. Have no fear: Jesus is with you, at this very moment, as I am writing, as you are reading these words. Don't lose faith, because I promise you that you are not alone.

Naturally I cannot share every experience I had, but I will highlight those times when I knew, without a shadow of a doubt, that Jesus had journeyed with me. These chapters will not be in chronological or even place order, so please read each chapter as a brand new ANYWHERE for me.

I will tell you, though, that I have travelled to five of the seven continents (excluding Africa and Antarctica) and have been to all of the fifty states. I have resided in nine different states for six months or more, and I have spent ten years of my journey overseas. Therefore, I enjoy travelling and going to wherever I feel the Lord has called me. In each chapter, I will identify each place so that you know the location of that particular ANYWHERE. God is so good to each one of us, and I am so thankful that in these few short years of my life, I can sing my favorite hymn with confidence, knowing that those words are ever so true. Be blessed, my friend, and know that wherever you are in your journey right now, the GOD of the universe is there with you, safely leading you to the next phase of your life. I don't know about you, but I cannot wait to see Jesus face-to-face and thank Him in person for safely leading me on this, my life's journey.

Special Thanks

I want to say a special thanks to our LORD and Savior Jesus Christ for giving me these experiences to share with you. My journey in life has been incredibly blessed and nothing would have been possible without HIM. To those earthly friends who financially contributed to all my travels, I must also say "thanks." To my mom and dad, Tom and Marlene Keaton, my Aunt Louesa Peters, my Aunt and Uncle Joan and Mardian Blair, and Fred and Georgia Land, who without even knowing it, made this all come together in the end. I also have to say a special thanks to ALL of you that provided me housing during my missionary journeys, abroad and in the states. Special thanks go to the late James and Robbie Lee Land, who allowed me to move in with them for six short months which turned into seven long, wonderful years. It is because of people like you that people like me can do what the Lord has called us to do. I have heard it said, and I believe it to be true, that those of us who are missionaries and in the overseas mission field, would be unable to do it without people like you who give so selflessly. Last, but definitely not least, I would like to say a BIG "thank you" to Beverly Gaines and Karla Spigner, for being an answer to my last prayers regarding this endeavor. This dream of mine to write down some of my experiences could not have been possible without the help of so many people. So, thanks to each one of you for helping to make my dream a reality. It is my hope and prayer that God will continue to bless you as you travel your life's journey.

Chapter 1

Did You See My Angel?

(Dirt Road Somewhere in Lafayette, Georgia)

It was a hot summer day, and I was the Bible worker for a small church in Lafayette, Georgia. I had received a request card from a lady who was interested in getting Bible study lessons. I got into my car with the hope that I would find her at home. I located her address on my map and began a journey that would forever impact my life. I was alone in my car, or so I thought, and after several minutes of driving, I realized that the road on which I was travelling was no longer paved but had become a narrow, red dirt road. I did not think much about it until I noticed that the houses were becoming fewer and further between—but the map I used as a guide seemed to show my destination to be right ahead!

> *I was alone in my car, or so I thought.*

As I travelled along, scanning the horizon for any sign of the lady's house, I noticed that there was one car ahead of me. By this time, the road was very narrow with nowhere to turn around. Soon the car in front of me began to slow down, and then it came to a complete stop, blocking my car. Anxiously I looked ahead and could see two men in the car, and when it stopped, one man got out and walked toward me. I was glad that my windows were rolled up, and then I thought, "This cannot be good. I am in the middle of nowhere, and nobody knows where I am, and there are two strange men, and one is approaching me." The man walking toward me loomed closer and closer, and then stopped at the hood of my car. At that moment I noticed he was looking toward my (what I thought was empty) passenger's seat, and his face took on a fearful appearance. He turned around as quickly as he could, got into his car, and sped off, blowing dust all the way down the road.

I have no idea who or what he saw that day, but there is one thing I do know—I was not alone during this encounter. The look on his face told me that, and the fact that he took off running to get away from me only confirmed in my mind the fact that he saw something I could not see: **my guardian angel**.

Does Jesus mean "anywhere" for you as well?

In 2 Kings 6 of the Holy Bible, there is a story about a time when Elisha the prophet was in trouble, and he knew, without even seeing, that there was a heavenly host of angels guarding him and his fearful men. When he prayed, he asked that their eyes be opened so that they could see what he knew in his heart was there already. When the Lord opened their eyes, their fears fell away as they saw the army of heavenly angels protecting them. As for me that day, on that lonely dirt road, I did not pray that the person whose possible intent could have been to harm me see the heavenly host—I simply prayed for God to protect me—but I do believe he did see someone or something that I could not. For that reason, he ran away. Therefore, my reminder for you today is that no matter where you are, you can with confidence hear the words in 2 Kings 6:16 which says, **"Fear not: for they that be with us are more than they that be with them."** If God could show Elisha a heavenly host of angels, and God could show the man that tried to harm me my guardian angel, He can surely do the same for you. The God of the Bible, who is the God of our lives, has a host of heavenly angels surrounding His people all over the world, helping them get to their next destination safely.

Chapter 2

The Ten-Minute Limousine Ride

(Interstate Highway Roadside Somewhere in Atlanta, Georgia)

If you have visited Atlanta, Georgia, you probably know that the traffic there is a nightmare! This was one of those times. My parents were driving me to the Atlanta airport for one of my many overseas trips. We had left home in enough time to make the international flight that day. My nephew, Corey, was with us, and we were approximately ten minutes from the airport—so close, in fact, that we could observe the planes taking off and landing. My dad was driving, and without warning, the car's "check-engine" light came on. He pulled over to the side of the very busy highway. The car engine quit, and my heart sank because I knew we were stuck and going nowhere. Even though we were within eyesight of the airport, I knew I did not want to walk that far with two huge pieces of luggage. My mother said a short prayer, and my dad got back into the car to say that he would walk to find some help. He started to open his car door when a long, black limousine pulled up beside us, and a voice from the driver's seat said, "Hurry up, get in! This is a very dangerous spot and we need to get you off the road, and fast." We all hurried to get my luggage and transferred it to the limousine, and a total stranger in a fancy car took us to the terminal, right on time. I do not know for sure, but sometimes I still wonder if that limousine driver was another angel. If not, I do believe that people can be angels in disguise. This is one time I can honestly say, "I rode to my destination in style!"

> *I do believe that people can be angels in disguise.*

Does Jesus mean "anywhere" for you as well?

On the morning of the day I left for the airport, "riding in style" was the furthest thing from my mind, but as I reflect upon this experience, I can see the goodness of God in not only getting me to the airport on time but also helping me realize that even when there is a crisis in life, He may surprise us with the ride of our lives. I have ridden in many cars in my lifetime but only in a limousine when there was a crisis. In many instances, I have seen the Lord use a crisis to get me to a better destination. Being stuck on the side of the road in Atlanta traffic was a crisis, but when God rescued us by sending a man in a limousine, it was no longer a crisis but an enormous blessing. Exodus 23:20 says, ***"Behold, I send an Angel before thee, to keep thee in the way, and to bring thee into the place which I have prepared."*** So just remember that wherever you are, angels go before you, to keep you, and to one day take you in style to that better place He has prepared.

Chapter 3

The Long Fall

(A Field Somewhere in Cohutta Springs Camp, State of Georgia)

One year while attending Fletcher Academy (a Seventh-day Adventist secondary school) in Fletcher, North Carolina, I had the privilege of attending a Bible retreat in Cohutta Springs. At the retreat, one of the activities was to climb over a twelve-foot wall with the assistance of fellow team members. The object was, as a united team, to get each team member to the top. I may have been the third or fourth person in line, and to my utter amazement, I made it. Once I got over the wall, there was a ledge on which to stand so that those of us that made it to the top could then help our oncoming teammates. When I got to the top of the wall, I was so excited that I did a very foolish thing: I forgot that I was twelve feet up in the air! I stepped backwards only to find that I was not on the ground (at least, not at that time). A few seconds later, I remember looking up and seeing many of my classmates surrounding me, asking if I were all right. I had landed on my back and for several minutes was so numb that I could not feel anything. After several more minutes, the staff decided that they would drive me home to Tennessee, where my family lived. Two strong men transported me to the school bus. I felt strange being in a huge bus with only two other people: the bus driver and the school's physical education teacher.

The ride to Collegedale, Tennessee, from Cohutta Springs, takes approximately 45 minutes, and we arrived as the sun was beginning to set. Unfortunately, when we pulled up, I saw that there was no car in the driveway, and I knew that my parents probably were not at home. After knocking on the door for several minutes, the physical education teacher realized that I was right—no one was home. We did not have cell phones in those days, so I was unable to call them to find out where they were.

Deciding what to do with me must have been a big frustration to those men. After several minutes of discussing what we should do, I suggested that they take me to my best friend's house located a few blocks down the street. My friend's mother was at home, and when she opened the door, they asked her if she knew me and whether she would be willing to allow me to remain at her house until my parents returned. She said of course I could stay, and once again, because I could not walk, these two men physically carried me into the house. An hour or so later we saw my parents drive past. Who knows what they thought when my friend told them to come to her house to pick me up ... after all, I was supposed to be away at school in North Carolina. The next day my mom took me to the doctor who diagnosed my injury as a torn knee ligament. Praise God that after several days of recuperation, I was back at the camp, hobbling along on crutches.

Does Jesus mean "anywhere" for you as well?

Proverbs 16:18 reminds me that *"Pride goeth before destruction, and an haughty spirit before a fall."* I can still remember how excited I was when I made it over that wall, and because of the excitement and my accomplishment of stepping onto that ledge, I allowed everything to overwhelm me. I forgot that I was still twelve feet off the ground. My pride for what I had accomplished overtook me that day, and because of that pride, I suffered a terrible fall. Have you asked yourself where you are today in your career, in your family life, in your church, or even in your own spiritual walk? Are you allowing pride to overtake you? And do you think constantly of all the great things that you have done? I believe it is wise that we check ourselves periodically to be sure our pride does not get in the way. As for me, my fall—both physically and spiritually—could have been disastrous. I thank God that when we do fall, He is beside us to help us get up. Wherever you are today, do not allow pride to overcome you. After all, none of us enjoys falling.

CHAPTER 4

A Long, Rainy Night

*(Somewhere on an Interstate Highway,
State of North Carolina)*

This experience took place when I was a student at Southern College in Collegedale, Tennessee. My parents lived in the community, and I lived with them while I went to school. However, most of my high school friends had to live on campus, and my home became a hangout for several of them. One vacation holiday a close friend asked me to go home with her. Her parents lived in Wilmington, North Carolina, so I was excited about going somewhere new, even though the trip would take approximately twelve hours. My friend said she would pick me up about nine o'clock that evening. We wanted to drive all night in order to have extra time to spend at the beach after arriving. When she picked me up, it was raining, and before we left, she asked my dad to check under the hood of the car to make sure that everything looked okay. He went out in the rain, lifted the hood, and within ten minutes, we were on our way. Another classmate was riding halfway with us, and we were to drop him off in Asheville, North Carolina. About midnight as we were driving along, the car started slowing down, making terrible noises, then it would speed up when we got to a level spot of road. Each time we drove up the slightest incline, the car slowed down dramatically and made weird noises. We all were afraid because we did not want to be stuck on the freeway at midnight in the rain. Somebody suggested we pray, so our classmate said a short prayer, and before he could say amen, the noises stopped and the car started to run normally—it was as though nothing had ever happened. An hour or so later, we arrived in Asheville and dropped off our rider. Early the next morning we pulled up to the home of my friend's mom and dad. We had almost forgotten about the problem with the car when her mother asked how her car had been doing at school. After hearing about how the car had acted on our trip, she suggested we take a nap while she took the car to the repair shop. She said she would be back in a couple of hours. By five o'clock that evening her mother had not returned, and we began to get a little worried. An hour or so later, she finally came home. We then asked her what took her so long, and she said that she barely made it to the repair shop. The car moved very slowly. When the mechanic at the shop checked under the hood, he asked her how long she had been driving the car in that condition. When she told the man that we had just driven all the way from Tennessee, he looked at her in disbelief, and said, "They couldn't have!" You have a busted head gasket, and you were lucky you could drive it even two miles. He told her that it was nothing short of a miracle. That evening, when we climbed into bed, we all said a special prayer of thanks to God for His amazing protection.

> *By five o'clock that evening her mother had not returned.*

Does Jesus mean "anywhere" for you as well?

After recounting this experience, I am again reminded that God hears prayers anytime and anywhere. This time for me, it had happened at midnight in a car, but for you it may be four o'clock in the morning, and you are in bed as you cry your last few tears. It may be ten o'clock in the morning at church service, or right now, as you face a major life decision. Whoever you are, wherever you are, never forget that God answers prayer. After all, Isaiah 65:24 says, *"And it shall come to pass, that before they call, I will answer; and while they are yet speaking, I will hear."* If it is true for me, it is surely true for you. Never forget that!!

Chapter 5

Surgery in North Carolina

(A Hospital Somewhere in North Carolina)

While in college, I had a friend who invited me to go home with her to North Carolina for spring break. The trip would take about twelve hours, and we would be gone for nearly ten days. We arrived at her home safely and had a great time. A few days after our arrival, I started to get a sore throat. I did not think much about it until I began to lose my voice. One night I was so miserable that I remember tossing and turning all night long. Early the next morning, I had completely lost my voice and my throat was hurting terribly. I decided that I had better ask her mom to take me to the doctor early that morning. She agreed to make an appointment for me.

When I went in to see the doctor, he told me to open my mouth to say "ah," but I was unable even to open my mouth. He had to stick an instrument inside of my mouth in order to pry it open for me. I was so surprised by his next comment. He said, "Your tonsils are really infected, and if you do not have surgery right away, you could die." He continued to explain, "We will schedule surgery for tomorrow morning." I could not believe it! I gave the doctor my mom's work phone number, as I was still a minor and knew that he needed to speak to her personally to get her permission to perform the surgery. My mom told me later that she almost hung up on the doctor because she thought the call was a wrong number. When she asked the caller, "Now, who did you say?" she realized that he was talking about me. She then gave consent for him to do the surgery.

> *It was not because they told me they loved me; it was because that day, they showed it.*

The next morning my tonsils were removed, and three or four hours later, I woke up. To my utter astonishment, my mother and father were sitting beside my bed. My mother said, "Are you alright?" I told her that I was and then drifted back to sleep. Later that afternoon, when I became more aware of my surroundings, I asked my friend if I had been dreaming about seeing my mother and father, and she said "no." She continued to explain that after my parents received the call that I was to have surgery, they got into their car and drove nearly 600 miles just to see if I was all right. Once they saw that I was ok, they got right back into the car and drove home. I have always known that my parents loved me, but this was one time I was sure of it. It was not because they told me they loved me; it was because that day, they showed it.

Does Jesus mean "anywhere" for you as well?

I often think about how our heavenly Father loves us so much that when we got in trouble He sent His Son, Jesus Christ, to this planet for a moment in time just to save us. Once He finished the job, by dying on the cross, He returned to His original home. If you always have known the love of the Father, praise God! But some of you may not know that love. Today, wherever you are, whoever you are, please be assured from the Word of God that He cares for and loves you very much. For me, John 3:16 and 17 prove this: *"For God so loved the world, that he gave his only begotten Son, that whosoever believeth in him should not perish, but have everlasting life. For God sent not his Son into the world to condemn the world; but that the world through him might be saved."* Please know that wherever you are today, your heavenly Father loves you very much, and He did the best thing He could to prove it. He not only says He loves us, but on that fateful Friday long ago, He proved it. Words were not enough!!

Chapter 6

The Lost Purse in Hawaii

(Bus Somewhere in Hawaii)

When I went to Southern Adventist University I wasn't sure what I wanted to study, so after two years of taking general classes, I decided that I wanted to try the student missionary thing for a year. This meant I would be spending the following school year overseas. I talked one of my friends into going with me, and so one day, we went to the Chaplain's office and looked through a large book describing all the places around the world where we could go to share our love for God to people who might never have heard of Him. After looking at our choices for a long time, we both decided that a tiny island called Truk, in the south Pacific, sounded like a great destination for adventure and opportunity. Before we finally left a few months later, we decided that it would be fun to go a week earlier than planned and do some sightseeing in Hawaii. Student missionaries from all around the world would be meeting in Hawaii for an orientation in the middle of August, and that seemed like a great opportunity to book an earlier flight and spend a week exploring on our own before our training date arrived.

Getting ready to move was so exciting. Neither my friend nor I had ever flown before, so going to the airport in Atlanta was a real thrill. Of course, tears began to flow when we finally had to say good-bye to our families, but once we got in the air, all the tears dried up, because we were finally off for a year of adventure!

When we finally landed in Hawaii, we almost had to pinch ourselves to be sure we were actually there, surrounded by the beautiful waters, the blowing palm trees, and the exotic birds and flowers. We had made arrangements beforehand to stay with a lady who rented out her home to travelers, so that was our first real experience of truly being on our own.

We did a lot of sightseeing during that week, and on one day in particular we decided to venture a little further out and take a bus to the other side of the island. When we finally arrived at our destination, we got off the bus and began to walk away, but then my friend Kim realized that she had left her purse on the bus. It contained all her money, her passport, and her other important papers. She started to run after the bus, but it was to no avail. We both stood there wondering what to do. One of us suggested that we pray about it. We had been watching the buses for a while, and we realized that each of them made a complete circle, and the bus on which we had ridden would return soon. After waiting on the roadside for almost an hour, we saw our bus. Kim eagerly boarded it and told the driver what she wanted. To my utter amazement, when she stepped off, there was a big smile on her face and her purse in her hand. Her purse had gone around the whole island with not one item missing from it. From that moment on, we knew that the two of us had not come alone but that Someone else had come along with us. We were so happy that we both prayed, thanking the Lord not only for protecting her purse but reminding us that He was with us.

Does Jesus mean "anywhere" for you as well?

Psalm 105:1, 2, tell us, *"O give thanks unto the LORD; call upon his name: make known his deeds among the people. Sing unto him, sing psalms unto him: talk ye of all his wondrous works."* There are several reasons why I wanted to write this book and share with you some of my experiences in life, but I think this text sums it up. We, as God's children, are to make known His deeds among the people, and talk of all His wondrous works. Today, as I write, and you read, I want to shout out what He has done for me. If God was good enough to bless us, He will certainly extend to you a blessing today. Wherever you are, it is time to shout out to others the marvelous deeds that He has done for you. You and I can never give Him enough praise for the things He has done.

Chapter 7

What Truk Did for Me!!!

(Somewhere on Truk Island, Now Known as Chuuk Island, Located in the Marshall Islands)

Before heading to Truk island, we had been informed that we were to meet student missionaries from all around the world in Hawaii for an orientation. After a week of training in Hawaii we were finally off to the Marshall Islands, where Truk is located. Along our route we made stops at several other islands.

The first stop was Johnston Island, an Air Force base. We were not allowed to leave the plane because this base was a major storage location of nerve gas. We were allowed to deplane at the next island of Majuro, however, for a few moments in order to stretch our weary legs. Next, we were off to Kwajalein, and the last stop of Pohnepi, before landing at Truk, our island home for the next year. When we finally saw the island where we would reside, my first thought was the landing strip was particularly short and should the pilot miss the landing, we could easily end up in the Pacific Ocean. It wasn't long before I actually found out how short it really was, because as we came in for the landing, I remember hearing the pilot announce over the intercom, "Sorry guys, we just missed our landing strip, and we have to try again." I think everybody cheered and clapped when he finally got it right the second time and the plane came to a stop.

One reason I had thought it would be fun to become a missionary was that I had the attitude that I was going to change the world, but little did I realize that this new world would change me. I would never be the same after this experience, because it was on the tiny little island of Truk in the South Pacific that I gave my heart totally and fully to the Lord. I had grown up in a wonderful loving family, but I had never really fallen in love with Jesus. I was just going through the motions. This changed, however, when I got to the place where the water catchment that supplied our water was located, and I realized that if we didn't get sufficient rainfall to fill it up, we would be in big trouble! I began to trust in the Lord like never before. Not having electricity for weeks was another faith builder, but it was not until that one unforgettable, eventful night when I knew what falling in love with the Lord really meant.

We had been on Truk for almost two weeks, and it was a Saturday night. The electricity had gone out—again—and it was getting dark. I remember thinking to myself, "Why in the world did you come out here? It is dark, hot, and too early to go to bed, and there is nothing to pass the time." I stepped outside on the ledge of our apartment and looked out into the ocean sky of stars. I thought, "I am so far away from my family and friends; yet God is SOOO good that He is watching over them just as He is me." I started to cry because it was then that I finally realized that JESUS really did love me, and He wanted to do something incredible in my life. My whole outlook on life changed in that instant because it was there that finally I realized God did have a purpose for my life, and it was to build my trust in Him and to learn how to serve others. After all, is not the Christian life about trusting GOD and serving others? At that moment in time, I decided that serving the Lord was something I wanted to do, and not because I had to. For those of us who have been Christians all our lives, we must at some point make this decision for ourselves. Now I can gratefully say that Truk Island is the place where God taught me this lesson.

Does Jesus mean "anywhere" for you as well?

If you are a Christian, you know that we all have our own conversion experience stories. Because we are all such diverse people with diverse experiences, God in His mercy gives each one of us a unique experience of the new life, or new birth. Even those of us who have been going to church with our parents since we were babes must have this experience for ourselves.

I remember being a young person attending church one Sabbath and thinking to myself that I was there on that day because churchgoing had become a habit. I really did not want to be there, but because I had done it all of my life, I continued. Later in my life, after the experience of working as an overseas missionary, John 4:41 and 42 became so real to me. It reads as follows: *"And many more believed because of his own word; And said unto the woman, Now we believe, not because of thy saying: for we have heard him ourselves, and know that this is indeed the Christ, the Savior of the world."* When I stepped out on that ledge that night and looked into the immense night sky, it was as though the Lord spoke to me from within all those stars. From that moment on, I decided I wanted to serve the Lord because I loved Him, not because I was forced to. In many instances we attend church only because it is the thing to do. Now when I attend church, I do so because that is what I desire to do and because I love the Lord. What about you? Are you doing things spiritually out of habit, or are you like the men and women of that town in the Bible who can honestly say, "Now we believe, not because of what you have said, but because of what we have heard ourselves"? Friend, wherever you are today, it is my prayer that you believe in Jesus, not because of what others have told you, but because you have heard Him yourself, and you too, can declare wherever you are that He indeed is the Christ, the Savior of the world. Prayerfully, serve Him because you love Him.

CHAPTER 8

Rain, Rain, Don't Go Away!!

(Somewhere on Truk Island)

Water can be a substance that many of us take for granted, but after my mission trip to Truk, I never looked at water in the same way. Our water supply came from a huge water catchment located on our school grounds. There were approximately twelve people who lived on the school compound, so this water catchment was the source of all of our water needs. During the rainy season, this was really not a problem since, as a rule, it would rain at least twice a day, filling up the catchment quite nicely; the dry season was another story.

Once my mom sent me a package, and inside was a package of grape Kool-Aid®. I remember one day that our water supply was dangerously low, and dirty water began to run from the faucet. I took my Kool-Aid® package and mixed it with the dirty water; in that way, I was unable see the dirt I was drinking. In many instances, we prayed for rain because we knew that if it did not come, we would have no water. Of course, God answered those prayers. I also remember all the times when we did have rain storms, that we stood under the rain gutters outside our apartment to shower. We did this because during the prior several weeks, we had been limited to sponge baths with only a bucketful of bath water. Water truly is a blessing from God!

Does Jesus mean "anywhere" for you as well?

Water is a necessity for every human being, for without it, eventually we would die. In Philippians 4:19 the Holy Bible says, *"But my God shall supply all your needs according to his riches in glory by Christ Jesus."* This text never meant more to me than when I knew that if the Lord didn't supply my need for water, I could die. Today as you think about where you are, stop for a minute and think about every need that you have at this moment. Then I want you to realize with me, that the Lord has already provided every need that you have. In fact, if He hadn't provided the air you needed this morning when you awoke, you would not be reading this book. You would no longer be alive. No matter where you are at this moment, PRAISE GOD that the basic needs you have for air, food, water, money, clothes, and health, have already been provided by the God who loves you. These are only a few of the requirements that we must have to survive, and PRAISE GOD that in His word, He has already promised to fulfill those needs for you today.

CHAPTER 9

A Truk Thanksgiving

(Somewhere on Truk Island)

I spent my first Thanksgiving overseas on Truk Island, and it is one I shall never forget. Every Thanksgiving I try to compile a gratitude list, and this one was no exception. In fact, I felt as though I had more bounteous blessings than usual.

The Friday before Thanksgiving, Truk was devastated by Typhoon Nina. Thanksgiving Day my roommate and I went to the local high school where hundreds of people were trying to get food relief. We handed out fruit baskets to everyone in need. Later that afternoon, in the pouring rain, we helped rebuild the home of one of our church members. Prior to the typhoon, the house was a tiny tin shack; after the typhoon, it had turned into broken heaps of tin. Within a few short weeks, the church member was living in a newly-constructed, concrete home.

> *It was on this Thanksgiving that I could attest to knowing what it means to be thankful.*

It was on this Thanksgiving that I could attest to knowing what it means to be thankful. This typhoon was so violent that it disabled all the electricity and phones on the island for more than a month. Additionally, we had no running water. This was one time where I felt severely isolated from the outside world. We could not communicate in any way, even by "snail mail," since the post office had no access to stamps. During this time, we were allowed only one bucketful of water per day for more than a month. Imagine how dirty we all felt! There were several times that I bathed in the local river where the island women washed their laundry, but I had to stop bathing there because I developed a rash. I was convinced that the rash came from my bathing downstream from the area where these women washed their dirty laundry.

A few weeks after the typhoon, there came another rainstorm, and that rain bath was absolutely wonderful. Of the many things to be thankful for each and every day of our lives, the miracle of water is among the most amazing, for without it we would die.

Does Jesus mean "anywhere" for you as well?

Psalm 107:1, 2 says *"O give thanks unto the LORD, for he is good: for his mercy endureth forever. (verse 2) Let the redeemed of the LORD say so, whom he hath redeemed from the hand of the enemy."* This text does not suggest that we give thanks only at Thanksgiving. I believe that the Lord would have us do this each and every day of our lives. Today, wherever you are, give thanks to the Lord, because He is good, ALWAYS. Often, we thank Him only once or twice a year on special occasions, but giving thanks to the Lord is an act He wants us to do as often as we have something to be thankful for, and is that not each day? Think about it—has He not been good to you today? No matter where you are, you can ALWAYS give Him thanks.

Chapter 10

Windows of Heaven

(A Kitchen on Truk)

My favorite passage of Scripture is Malachi 3:10, which states that we are to return our tithes and offerings and see if the Lord will not throw open the windows of heaven for us when we do. The reason that this verse is so very special to me is that in following it, I can take Him at His Word.

At this time, student missionaries were making approximately $200 a month, which was quite sufficient for our needs. One Sabbath the pastor made an offering appeal and asked us to put the Lord to the test. He informed us that the following Sabbath would be the yearly annual sacrifice offering in which the churches were asking all their members to give half of their paycheck. After the service, my roommate and I considered it. Eventually we decided that if we pooled our resources and each of us gave $100, there would still be $200 between us. Besides, we lived on an island, and we knew we could catch some ocean fish or climb up a coconut tree if we had to. We were certain that we would not go hungry. On the next Sabbath, reluctantly, we each gave $100.

> *Truly God's timing is perfect, and His Word can be trusted.*

The following Monday morning my roommate came running into my class yelling, "Guess what, guess what? My mom sent us a package of fifty pounds worth of American food." (Little Debbie® Cakes and canned vegetarian food never tasted so good!) The next day, my mom sent a twenty-pound package of food. Later that week as we were storing this abundance of food in our small kitchen cupboards, we realized that our kitchen was too small for all the food; we had to store supplies in our bedroom. Not only that, but at the end of the month, neither of us had spent a penny of that $100 that we had not given.

The real miracle, though, came when we just happened to look at the date that my roommate's mom sent the package. Her mom had told us that she mailed that package first class from America so that it would be shipped by plane, but when we looked at the postmark date on the package, we realized that it had been mailed three months earlier and had traveled by boat across the Pacific Ocean. Truly God's timing is perfect, and His Word can be trusted.

Does Jesus mean "anywhere" for you as well?

When the Word of God in Scripture speaks to you personally, it truly makes the Bible come alive and it is when God's promise in His Word comes true, you know, without a doubt, what He says is real. For me, Malachi 3:10 is that Word which says, *"Bring ye all the tithes into the storehouse, that there may be meat in mine house, and prove me now herewith, saith the LORD of hosts, if I will not open you the windows of heaven, and pour you out a blessing, that there shall not be room enough to receive it."* When we received that package that day and I put all that food in my bedroom because my cupboards in the kitchen would not hold the food, it was at that moment that His still small voice said to me, "This is what I am talking about. You did prove Me, as I said you should, and now the floodgates of heaven have been opened for you." I cannot honestly say I have never thought about robbing God again since then, but it is at the times when I do, He reminds me of this experience and I must say to myself, "Are you kidding? After the many blessings He has given me, why would I want to take what is rightfully His?" I challenge you to re-visit Malachi 3:10, and see if the God of the universe will not throw open the floodgates of heaven for you. Just remember, though, it may not come in the form of money because at that time, I didn't need money, I needed food. Wherever you are God's blessings can come in many different ways.

Chapter 11

No Knees on Sokez Rock

(Somewhere on Sokez Rock, Pohnpei)

During a Christmas break, I decided to visit some friends on the island of Pohnpei, which was only an island away. On New Year's Day that year, ten of us decided to hike up Sokez Rock, the highest mountain on Pohnpei. I have never been much of a hiker, but I decided to go anyway, since I had heard it would be an experience I would never forget. After much persuading, reluctantly I decided to go. We hadn't gone very far, when my legs began to rebel with each step, but I ignored the threats of my body. "Just a little farther," I kept telling myself. Finally, as I crested the top behind the others, I sucked in my breath at the absolutely spectacular view. I felt like I was on top of the world, and all I could see was the brilliant blue Pacific Ocean. The tropical water reflected the blue sky, and as I watched birds flying off in the distance, I felt almost birdlike at my perch on top of the world. The whole group sat reverently admiring the panoramic view as we rested for a while.

> *"Just a little farther," I kept telling myself.*

When it was time to go, I attempted to stand up, but my knees failed me, and I could not stand. Frightened, I tried to get up again. Over and over I tried, but each time, my legs crumbled beneath me. I could not stand, no matter how hard I tried. It was as if my knees had just disappeared, and every time I tried to stand, I would fall again. There was a very strong Pohnpeian man in our group, who, when he saw my predicament and fear, literally picked me up and carried me down the mountain on his shoulders. I have never been a small person, so I am sure he had no idea as to what his actions would require of him. I was greatly relieved until I remembered all that we had traversed to get to the top. Going in reverse, downhill, on top of his shoulders was very scary. It was difficult to sense which side of his torso to lean on as he stepped here and there, so I just hung on tightly. The most frightening part was sitting on his shoulders while he walked on a log over a ravine as we crossed to the other side of the cliff. After several hours, we arrived safely, and I was never happier to be on solid ground. It literally took three days for me to walk normally again.

Does Jesus mean "anywhere" for you as well?

In this life, we all have problems. When we get to the point where we realize that we cannot do something on our own, it is then, that I believe the Lord wants to remind us that He is there to carry us to a more solid ground. I know for certain, that without this man's help, I would not have been able to get to the bottom that day. I had continued to struggle on my own, but I kept falling. Isaiah 35:3, 4 says, *"Strengthen ye the weak hands, and confirm the feeble knees. Say to them that are of a fearful heart, Be strong, fear not: behold, your God will come with vengeance, even God with a recompence; he will come and save you."* This text reminds me that when we fall, and our knees are weak, He will be there to help us. Since the problems we have on this earth can be devastating at times, this text also reminds me that we are to be strong, because HE is strong, and He promises to one day come and save us. Praise God, that like the strong Pohnpeian man that carried me to level ground, we can always rely on our heavenly Father to carry us on His shoulders to get us to our final destination.

Chapter 12

Will I Ever Get Clean Again?

(Somewhere on Pohnpei, Marshall Islands)

One of the first things I had to get used to in Truk was taking cold showers. We had no hot water since the water that we relied on had originated from the rain and was stored in the water tank—and it did not go through a water heater! This was not as bad as it may sound, though, because it was always hot in Truk. Sometimes a cold shower was a relief, but at other times, a hot shower would have been such a blessing.

The amount of water we could use was quite limited because the compound where I lived housed at least twelve other missionaries, and all of us had to rely upon the same water in the catchment. For months each of us was limited to using one bucket of water for bathing. After a while, this became just a normal routine. It was almost Christmas when I decided to visit some friends who lived on the island of Pohnpei, an island away from Truk. Fortunately, Pohnpei was somewhat more modern than Truk in that standard showers did exist there. Upon my arrival, one of the first things that I did was to take a real shower; it was a fairly short one, and when I finished, my friend asked, "Why did you take such a quick shower?"

I said, "because the water is so cold." She said, "Why didn't you turn on the hot water?"

"Oh, you have hot water? In that case, I will take another one," I replied. I think I took about five or six showers that day because it felt so good to have all that hot water run over my dirty body. It wasn't until a few days later that I finally decided that I had had enough steaming showers in that wonderful hot water!

> **For months each of us was limited to using one bucket of water for bathing.**

Does Jesus mean "anywhere" for you as well?

When I think about all the showers I took that day in Pohnpei, I am reminded of Jeremiah 2:22. It says, *"For though thou wash thee with nitre, and take thee much soap, yet thine iniquity is marked before me, saith the Lord GOD."* No matter how many showers I took that day, I never felt clean. Just the other day, I was retelling this experience to my friend whose house I had visited in Pohnpei, and she reminded me that what she found interesting about this was the fact that not only did I take many showers, but every time I took another shower I also had to wash my hair. I must have washed my hair six times because every part of my body felt dirty. No matter how many showers I took, I never felt totally clean. As I relate this to Jeremiah 2:22, I am reminded that nothing but the blood of Jesus can cleanse my filthy soul from sin. No matter how many times I try to clean myself up, I will always feel dirty. This is exactly how I felt in Pohnpei. Spiritually speaking, water will never totally cleanse me; it is only the blood of Jesus that will make me clean, and yet no matter how I try, my sin(s) will remain there until I cover myself with His blood. Water will never do the trick, so no matter where you are today, no matter what you do, or have done, don't try to cleanse yourself with water, but cover yourself with His blood, because water alone will never do the trick.

Chapter 13

God's Perfect Timing

(Began Somewhere in Tennessee—Ended Somewhere in Guam)

Culture shock was not something that I felt like I really experienced when I travelled overseas. For me, though, reverse cultural shock was terrible. I had a hard time readjusting to American life after spending nearly two years on a small island. When I returned to America I can remember one Friday evening just sobbing to my mother that I just didn't know how to readjust to the American way of life. My mother tried to comfort me but had a hard time. During our discussion she said, "If you loved being overseas so much, why don't you go to a college overseas and finish your education there?" She also reminded me that I had a friend who was living in Guam, and she suggested that I check out the university there. (For her to suggest that was where this miracle began because I didn't even know she had heard of Guam.) That sounded like a great idea!

A few days later, I bought a one-way ticket to Guam.

It was nearly 8 p.m. and I decided that it would be a great time to call my friend and with the time zone difference, she probably would be getting up to go to church. I found her number and after a few short rings she answered the phone. After a few minutes of small talk she said, "You don't want to go to school, you want to teach, right?"

I said, "Sure, if I knew where to go".

"We have a position open for a seventh-grade teacher at our school, Guam Adventist Academy." She then asked, "How soon can you get here?" Without thinking I told her I could leave as soon as I got a ticket. "Great!" was her reply and she hung up the phone.

A few days later, I bought a one-way ticket to Guam. Unbeknownst to me at the time, the Lord had allowed me to find seventy dollars the week before. After finding it, I put it in a savings account. When I went to purchase my plane ticket to Guam, there was one dollar more in the account than the ticket cost. It was then that I knew why I had found that seventy dollars!

When I arrived in Guam the day before Thanksgiving and heard my friend's version of the story, I knew without a doubt that this is where the Lord wanted me to be. She told me that the day before I called, she was teaching grades seven and eight and had just experienced a really horrible day; that night she had prayed that the Lord would find a teacher by Monday morning; otherwise, she had told the Lord, that she was going to hand her in resignation. She went to sleep that night, and early the next morning I called to say that I was available to teach. This then began a new journey for me where I spent the next year teaching the seventh-grade at Guam Adventist Academy.

Does Jesus mean "anywhere" for you as well?

With this particular experience, Ecclesiastes 3:11 says it all. *"He hath made everything beautiful in his time: also he hath set the world in their heart, so that no man can find out the work that God maketh from the beginning to the end."* The Lord really does make everything beautiful in His time. I look at this experience and cannot help but think how true this is. Everything in this incident fit in perfect alignment with His perfect plan for my life at that time. My experience in Guam was so wonderful, not just because of the place, not just because of the people, but because I knew without a doubt that I was exactly where God wanted me at that moment. Some of you may not know what the Lord is doing in your life right now, but if you don't have peace about where you are, maybe it could be that you are not exactly where God wants you to be. I suggest you pray about where you are and then ask Him to show you if He is making everything beautiful in HIS time. Wherever you are today, thank the Lord for His beautiful timing in your own life. Who knows? Perhaps you are where you are because He has put you there for His purpose right now, today.

Chapter 14

Typhoons

(Somewhere on the Island of Guam)

While living on Guam, I experienced many more typhoons than I had on Truk Island. I am very grateful that the houses in Guam were more able to withstand the storms. For those of you that don't know, a typhoon is a storm that originates over the Pacific Ocean, much like a hurricane is a storm originating over the Atlantic. One year we had about six typhoons within three short months.

I remember one particular storm which the media reported would be quite weak and that we should not be concerned about it. No one did anything to prepare for the storm. Unfortunately, this was one of the worst typhoons ever to have hit Guam. Fortunately, even though we had been falsely warned, nobody lost their life. A week or so later, they told us that another storm was coming and that it was going to be a big one. This one, however, never came. But you can be assured that this time everybody was ready. For the next two or three months, we were threatened by storms quite often. People began to leave their window shutters on for weeks at a time. It was just too much work to take them off only to have to put them back up a week later. We were all thrilled when that typhoon season was finally over.

> *You can be assured that this time everybody was ready.*

Does Jesus mean "anywhere" for you as well?

Matthew 24:42 tells us to *"Watch therefore: for ye know not what hour your Lord doth come."* When I think about all the storms in Guam, it reminds me of the second coming of Christ. If you are a Christian, you probably have heard of His second coming most of your life. We all should know that this event is eminent, but we also need to ask ourselves, "Are we prepared?" This is like my first experience with a storm in Guam where we were told it was nothing to worry about and then it turned into one of the worst storms Guam had experienced. The second time, we were told it would be a "Big One" and nothing happened. Soon after that we were ready all the time. Because of this I am trying to live my life ALWAYS READY! I know it is coming, so I have decided to try my best to be ready all the time. Just like the people in Guam who left up there shutters all the time, I know I should be ready all the time. Wherever you are today, ask yourself how ready am I for the Lord to come? Should He come today, would you be ready? If not, don't you think it's about time to get ready? With all the signs around us, I'm certain that He is on His way, ready or not!!

A storm is coming. Are you ready?

CHAPTER 15

The Mute Second Grader

(Classroom in Guam)

My second year in Guam I was told that I would be teaching second grade. The summer before I began to teach, I asked the first-grade teacher to tell me a few things about this particular class of would-be second graders that I would have the following year. In our conversation, she spoke of a little girl in the class who would not talk. She informed me that this girl had been diagnosed as "elective mute." This meant that she would choose to whom she talked and speak only to them. For the past two years she had not spoken to any of her teachers. I thought that things would change after she came to know me, but it did not. Little *Kate* just would not talk to me. As you can imagine, I was quite frustrated. After the Thanksgiving holiday, the school hired a child psychologist to work with her a few times a week outside the classroom. That was also to no avail. I don't remember who suggested this, but when I told them about Kate, they suggested that I not only pray for her, but with her, so that she could actually hear me pray for her.

One sunny Sunday, I decided to take Kate to the beach. Her psychologist went with us, and we had a lovely day playing in the water and building sandcastles. We tried everything we could do to get her to talk to either one of us, but she would not respond. At the end of the day, Kate still was silent. Before we left, I took her by the hand and said a prayer for her, asking the Lord to help her to talk, but still no words came from her mouth. Naturally, I left the beach disappointed that she had not spoken. For the next few weeks, I took her out of the classroom each day and prayed with her. A few weeks before the school

> *Before we left, I took her by the hand and said a prayer for her.*

year ended I became real discouraged over the situation, because I knew that the year would soon be over and Kate had still not spoken. One day *Sarah*, the child psychologist, took Kate out as usual, and about fifteen minutes later, I heard a knock on the door. It was Sarah. She said, "Kate has something she wants to say to you." I got down on my hands and knees and with a little prompting, Kate whispered the most beautiful words I have ever heard. She said, "Hello, Miss Keaton." Tears came to my eyes. "Hello" never sounded so good! Kate did not say much else to me that year, but that was okay, because hello was all I needed. The following year her new teacher said that Kate talked up a storm. I thank God often that He is still in the miracle working business.

** Pseudonyms used

Does Jesus mean "anywhere" for you as well?

There is a story in Mark 7:31–37 about a man who could not talk, and Jesus came to town one day and cured him. It reads as follows: ***"And again, departing from the coasts of Tyre and Sidon, he came unto the sea of Galilee, through the midst of the coasts of Decapolis. And they bring unto him one that was deaf, and had an impediment in his speech; and they beseech him to put his hand upon him. And he took him aside from the multitude, and put his fingers into his ears, and he spit, and touched his tongue; And looking up to heaven, he sighed, and saith unto him, Ephphatha, that is, Be opened. And straightway his ears were opened, and the string of his tongue was loosed, and he spake plain. And he charged them that they should tell no man: but the more he charged them, so much the more a great deal they published it; And were beyond measure astonished, saying, He hath done all things well: he maketh both the deaf to hear, and the dumb to speak."*** The lesson for me in this is very obvious. We serve a God who still works miracles, and He does it anywhere and everywhere. Wherever you are today, remember that you still can call on the God of the universe who cares about His children and their needs. If He can cause a man to speak and hear in biblical times, and He can cause a mute second-grader to speak in Guam, He can surely help you. With Kate, though, her speech did not come immediately after prayer because I prayed for her almost a whole year; when I finally heard her voice for the first time, it was as though the Lord told me that my persistent prayers were what He wanted from me. My friend, keep praying for that miracle to come because, in many instances, persistence is what He requires to test our faith in Him.

CHAPTER 16

Does God Have a Sense of Humor?

(On a Busy Highway in Hawaii)

We all have our own opinion of God, but there are times when I really believe that God must have a sense of humor, and this experience is one of those times when I am sure that God must have been laughing with me. I have an aunt who decided to take a trip to meet me in Hawaii for some vacation time.

The one thing that will always stand out about this trip for me occurred when we were driving to the airport to fly to one of the smaller islands. We had rented a car and were sitting in traffic, and I was admiring the scenery around us when suddenly I looked at the bus next to us and yelled, "I can't believe it!" I started waving my arms and my aunt must have thought I was going nuts because she did not realize what I was doing, but this was because I recognized a person sitting on the bus as a doctor friend of mine. I had met him several years ago when I was a student missionary on Truk Island. *Dale* was an American man that had been a missionary doctor on Truk Island with me several years before. I was amazed because when I started waving my arms around to catch his attention, he looked over at me, stood up, went to the front of the bus and asked the bus driver to let him off. He then proceeded to run down the busy traffic lanes to our car.

After my aunt found a place to pull over, he jumped in the car, and what a grand reunion we had! He informed us that he was then living in Hawaii and was en route to work that morning. He told us how a few minutes before that he had been sitting on the aisle seat and the girl next to the

> **I really believe that God must have a sense of humor.**

window got off the bus. Normally he would not have moved over, but this particular morning he felt a strong urge to move over to the window seat. A few minutes after he moved over, he looked over at the car next to him, and saw this strange person (me) waving her arms wildly in the air. I am certain that God had ordained all of our steps that morning. Talk about being in the right place at the right time—this was definitely one of those times.

** Pseudonym used

Does Jesus mean "anywhere" for you as well?

Ecclesiastes 3:4 says that there is *"… A time to weep, and a time to laugh; a time to mourn, and a time to dance."* Have you ever had an experience that often brings joy to your life when you think back upon it? There are times when I look back in my life and remember with awe what God has done, and when I think about meeting my friend on the highway in Hawaii, I can't help but laugh. I can still see him jumping off that bus onto the busy highway and into our car with us. I think of all the space in the world, and yet how God in His wisdom put us both at the same spot at the same time. So yes, I do believe, as Solomon said, that there is a time to laugh, and I believe that when we laugh, He laughs with us. Wherever you are today, my friend, take time to laugh at some of the ways that God has done something extraordinarily special for you. Surely life can and will be tough, but I am certain that at some of the places along your journey, you, too, can find something to laugh about. I have no idea why the Lord wanted me to see my friend that day, but who knows? Maybe it was because He knew we all needed a good laugh, and to remind us that He is the One who directs our steps.

Chapter 17

The Long Way to Nowhere

(Somewhere in Busan, South Korea)

Have you ever had something in your life that was frustrating at the time, but quite funny after the situation was over? Well, this is just one such incident. After leaving Guam, I went to Busan, South Korea where I taught at an English language school. One day a friend rode a train from Seoul to Busan, where I lived. He was in the military and wanted me to take him to a car auction at the military base in Busan. I was not sure of the route, so I asked one of my Korean students how to get there. The student said, "take Bus #10 and then Bus #16." I was sure that I knew what we were doing. After all, getting on only two buses could not be that difficult, could it?

We left a few hours early so that we could get to the auction on time. We caught Bus #10 and rode around, perhaps for an hour or so; then the bus came to a parking lot and everybody told us to get off. We then saw Bus #16, so we got on it; during the entire time, we were both thinking that we were merely transferring. After about a half an hour, things began to look strangely familiar. My friend said, "Doesn't that look like the same building we passed on the other bus?" I said, "No, it can't be." After another half an hour, we had arrived at our starting location. We both laughed when we realized what had happened. My student had forgotten to tell us where to get off Bus #10. Bus #16 was the one we were to catch for our return trip. By this time, it was late in the day; so, my friend had to call for a taxi and we got to the base just in time for the place to close. My friend was not very happy, but he knew that getting angry would not change things; he asked around and found out that the auction was to continue the next day. Early the next day, he arrived at the auction only to be disappointed because he did not find a car. Neither one of us ever figured out why we took the wrong bus that day, but maybe it was because we were to appreciate the humorous things in life, even in the most frustrating situations. At the time, it was anything but funny, but when I look back on it, I can't help but have a good laugh.

Does Jesus mean "anywhere" for you as well?

Proverbs 16:9 says, *"A man's heart deviseth his way: but the LORD directeth his steps."* This is one of those times that I must say I wonder why in the world it happened the way that it did, and then after reading this text, I cannot help but be reminded that for whatever reason, the Lord was still directing our steps. My friend had an agenda that day, but in reality, it was the Lord who directed us. For both of us, it seemed like a wasted day in our eyes, yet God's plan is perfect and even if we can't see it, He has a reason for everything. Although we don't know the "why," there was one and it was to remind me that the Lord is the One who ultimately directs our steps. My friend, wherever you are today, remember that you may plan your day and your ways, but in the end, it is really the Lord who will direct your steps for this day. Whether or not you see the point, the Lord ultimately directs your path.

CHAPTER 18

To Tell the Truth

(Somewhere in China)

Before going to Mainland China, we had a training orientation in Hong Kong. While I was there I met another American lady about my age, and she was assigned to the same University where I was going. Her name was Laurie, and I was so glad that she would be traveling with me, because she had just spent a year in Taiwan, and could speak fluent Mandarin Chinese. I knew having her as a co-missionary would be an awesome thing since she would be able to understand the language. While in training we were warned to be careful when speaking about spiritual matters, since China is still a Communist country. We were also told that we could take as many Chinese/English Bibles with us as we could fit into our suitcases, so Laurie and I grabbed as many Bibles as we could fit into our bags. We then said a word of prayer, asking the Lord to help us get them into China safely.

The next day Laurie and I boarded the plane and everything went well—at first. During our flight, however, the stewardess came around with some paperwork asking us to declare everything we were taking into the country. Naturally one of the questions was, "Do you have any printed religious material?" We had to make a decision to lie or tell the truth. If we lied and they caught us, we could be in some serious trouble; but I also knew that if we told the truth and we got caught, they would probably kick us out of the country before we even got in. I knew what we had to do, so we checked the box that said we were bringing in Bibles. When the plane landed we said an extra prayer and decided that it would be best if we got off the plane last so that if we were detained, we would not detain others. We were the last two to get off the plane, and when we got inside, the security guards were going through everybody's luggage piece by piece. I just knew we were in trouble. It was almost our turn and I heard one of the guards say something in Chinese to another guard and then leave. Then the guy that was left motioned for us on through. We walked through the line without their even looking at the contents of our luggage. I found out later that the other guard had told his friend he was tired and needed a break. I thank God for His providence and care that day!

Does Jesus mean "anywhere" for you as well?

The ninth commandment, found in Exodus 20:16, says, ***"Thou shalt not bear false witness against thy neighbour."*** Basically, it tells us that we should not lie. I am so glad that I decided to tell the truth, and that I trusted God to take care of the rest. In many instances people lie so that they will not get into trouble, but after this experience, I am a firm believer that if we tell the truth, the Lord will bless us and help us avoid trouble. I also thank God that on this day we were impressed to let others go first. Had we decided not to let the other passengers off the plane first, I am certain that our luggage would have been checked. My message to you is, wherever you are, lying is never a wise alternative. I know from experience that when we tell the truth and honor God, He will honor us for our faithfulness. Each time I gave away one of those Bibles in China, I was so thankful that the Lord had helped me tell the truth on that airplane. I cannot wait to get to heaven and hear about how those Bibles made a difference in someone's life, all because my friend and I decided to follow one of God's commandments and not lie.

Chapter 19

Angel in the Rice Paddy

(Rice Paddy in Zigong, China)

One Sabbath afternoon Laurie and I decided to walk through the Chinese rice paddies not far from our guest house, to visit with some farmer friends she had met a few days earlier. I told her I would go if we could return before dark. Laurie and I had a nice visit with the farmers and about 6 o'clock we decided that it was time to head home. Laurie had walked quite a distance ahead of me when all of a sudden I fell and somehow my foot got stuck in a hole. I was stuck in the hole and was unable to get out. My friend tried to twist and turn my foot, but unfortunately I was really stuck, and I was going nowhere fast.

> *I was really stuck, and I was going nowhere fast.*

Had my foot not become stuck, however, I am certain I would have fallen into the very wet rice paddy below. While glad that that hadn't happened, unfortunately I wasn't able get my foot out of the hole. I yelled at my friend to help me, and of course she tried, but her effort was futile.

After trying again and again, we decided that she should go back to the university and get help before dark. She was almost out of my sight when I decided to pray. I could see the sun setting and knew that she would have a hard time getting back before the darkness fell, and I was afraid. A few minutes after I prayed, I literally felt an unseen hand twist my foot, and it came out of the hole without any problem. I jumped up and ran to catch up with my friend. She was so surprised to see me and became overjoyed when I told her that my guardian angel, whom I did not see, pulled my foot out of that hole. Praise the Lord, we arrived back home before the sun set.

Does Jesus mean "anywhere" for you as well?

The day my foot became stuck in that hole, and my guardian angel helped me out, I was reminded of another one of my favorite verses in Psalms 34:7. It says, *"The angel of the LORD encampeth round about them that fear him, and delivereth them."* Although I was unable to physically see my angel that day, I know what I felt, and I am certain I felt the hand of my angel release me from that hole. As my friend was leaving to return to the university for help, I must admit, I was scared and wondered if she would return before dark. It was when I said a prayer for help that I felt my angel's presence. There are many times in our lives when we wait until we are afraid before crying out for help. All I know is that I was so happy when my help came that day. My friend, no matter where you are today, do not wait until you become afraid to call for help. Call for help the minute you need it. This text reminds us that our angels are always around us, waiting to deliver us from the hand of the enemy. We all need help at times in our lives, and when you do, remember that your angels are willing and waiting whenever you call.

Chapter 20

This Is Not Our Home

(University in Sichuan China)

Upon our arrival in China, Laurie and I were assigned to teach English at Sichuan Institute of Light Industry and Chemical Technology. The school where we taught was in Zigong, China, in the province of Sichuan. Laurie and I lived in a small, hotel-style apartment complex. This was basically a guest house that housed foreign teachers and guests of the University. It was located at the far side of the campus where there was a wall, and outside the wall were rice paddies. To get to our classrooms every day we had to cross the residential part of the University campus—the apartments and buildings which housed teachers and staff members. Just before we reached the main campus we had to pass the school nursery, a one-story building with big windows. The only route to our classrooms required us to walk past this school nursery where the faculty children were enrolled in school during the day while their parents were teaching.

Each day we walked past the nursery and, regardless of what they were doing, the minute they saw my missionary friend and me, the children began to chant and yell, "Wàiguórén, Wàiguórén" (which means "foreigner" in English). Some afternoons I felt sorry for these children, because if even one child was awake at naptime, he or she would begin to chant this phrase and awaken all the others. It was a bit comical at first but became a real nuisance for the nursery workers. As soon as one child said the word, all the others would chant it. I started to hate walking past the nursery knowing that at any moment one of those children would see me.

One day as they were chanting, my friend made an excellent observation. She said, "You know, whenever they yell 'foreigner' at us, this should remind us that we really are all foreigners." After thinking about her statement, I realized that each day the Lord was reminding me that indeed I am a foreigner, no matter where I am.

Does Jesus mean "anywhere" for you as well?

Since there was only one route to work, we had no choice except to walk past that nursery each time we needed to get to class. After hearing the chant multiple times, it really did become quite annoying because even if only one kid saw us, the whole group stood, looked out the window, and chanted until we passed. One day the Lord reminded me of how true this is. We are all foreigners here. There is only one way to get to heaven, and praise the Lord, He wants to remind us of that each day. Hebrews 11:16 says, ***"But now they desire a better country, that is, an heavenly: wherefore God is not ashamed to be called their God: for he hath prepared for them a city."*** Wherever you are today, remember earth is not your home. You may call it home, but the Lord wants to remind us often that He is preparing a much better place for us, and we are just passing through this realm. I am awed with how He sent me all the way to another country to remind me that wherever I am on this planet, I am merely a foreigner. This earth is a temporary place of residence for me because our ultimate home is a place called heaven. I do not know about you, but one day very soon, I am going home. I praise God often that He used a group of Chinese kindergarteners to teach me this very important lesson. You and I are truly "Wàiguóréns" no matter where we are.

CHAPTER 21

The Thanksgiving Bag

(Field in China)

My first Thanksgiving in China was one that I shall never forget. I had wanted to do something special for an impoverished native Chinese person, so I decided to make a Thanksgiving basket of fruit. I asked my Foreign Affairs Officer to go out to the countryside with me to give the basket to a needy person. I did not have a basket so I decided to look through my drawer for a bag. I found that I had saved a nice sturdy bag with a beautiful picture on the front that I had brought from America. My first thought was that I might keep it for some special occasion. Then I decided that since I was leaving soon, and this could be considered a special occasion, I decided to go ahead and use it. I placed the fruit in the bag, and the two of us walked in the direction of the Chinese countryside.

We had not gone very far when my Foreign Affairs Officer said, "What about her?" She was one of the ladies who came by our garbage bin outside of our hotel and picked up our "good" trash every day. I said "ok." We then walked over to her, and I handed her the bag full of all kinds of wonderful fruit. At first she did not want to accept it, but after my Foreign Affairs Officer explained to her about American Thanksgivings, she took it. Before she did though, she looked at the Foreign Affair Officer and said, "You mean I can keep the bag too?" I said of course, and tears came to her eyes. I could see that the bag was more precious to her than was the fruit because she could probably sell the bag and earn a good day's wages from it. I thought about that experience and I felt so ashamed for wanting to keep the best bag for myself. I had not realized the bag would mean more to her than what was in it.

Does Jesus mean "anywhere" for you as well?

1 King 10:18 says, *"Moreover the king made a great throne of ivory, and overlaid it with the best gold."* This text says that King Solomon not only made a throne of ivory, but that he overlaid it with the best gold. He did not use regular gold—he used the best gold that he could find. After the experience with the farmer lady in China, I now ask myself, why is it that when He asks us for something, we often want to give Him our second best? Why is it that we have so much to be thankful for, yet we always want to keep the best for ourselves? That day, I really thought about just putting the fruit in a big ugly brown paper bag and using the pretty colorful bag to carry my belongings back to America. After seeing this poor Chinese lady shed tears because she realized she could keep the bag *and* the fruit, I was so ashamed of myself. I wanted to do something nice for somebody, yet I wanted to keep the nicest bag for myself. I did not realize the bag was more precious to the lady than was the fruit.

There are many times when we are selfish about saving the best for ourselves. It's the natural thing for us to do. But God asks us to give of ourselves and to give our best. Today, wherever you are, think about the things that you give to others and see if you have a habit of keeping the best for yourself. That means that you give Jesus your second best. My friends, this should not be, because if we are thankful for the best gift Jesus gave us, Himself, why would we want to give Him our second best?

CHAPTER 22

Meet My Chinese Angel

(Yantai, Shandong Province, China)

I lived in Sichuan, a province of southern China, for a year. At the end of the school year, I was asked to make a job transfer to Shandong province in northern China. Before accepting the call, I decided to visit the school in Shandong to be able to make an informed decision. The trip required that I take a six-hour train ride, a three-hour plane ride, and then another train ride. I talked my Foreign Affairs Officer into accompanying me on the first train ride. I was thrilled to have her with me since my Chinese was not very good. During our six-hour ride she gave me a note written in Chinese with the instructions that I was to give to the taxi driver once I got off the airplane. The note was written so that the taxi driver would take me to a local hotel, where I could rest until having to catch my next train the following morning.

Once we got off the train, we got in a local taxi, and headed for the airport. After arriving there, she helped me onto the plane, and then we said our goodbyes. I was tired and hoped that the plane was not full so that I would have room to rest. Unfortunately for me, it was a packed flight. As the plane began to fill up, a young Chinese man sat down beside me, and I thought to myself, "Oh no, I am sure I will not rest on this trip." I had lived in China long enough to know that most Chinese like to talk to foreigners, so I automatically thought that my opportunity to get some rest was now gone. It happened just as I thought, and he began talking to me. I was surprised, though, at how good his English really was. As we talked, and I told him I was on my way to Yantai, he asked me where I was spending the night and how I was going to catch a taxi since I could not speak much Chinese. I showed him the note my Foreign Affairs Officer had written and explained that she had told me to give it to the taxi driver when I got there. The man beside me said, "I can do better than that. How about letting me help you catch a taxi? I can tell him where you want to stay for the night." I said, "That would be awesome." When the plane landed he said, "Follow me."

We exited the plane and he took me outside where the taxis were waiting for potential passengers. He called a taxi and spoke to the driver in Chinese; then he motioned me to get into the taxi. As we pulled away, the young man looked me right in the eyes and said, "Be safe." I turned around to say thank you and immediately saw my new Chinese friend vanish into thin air! I arrived at my destination safely, knowing that the Lord had just sent my guardian angel to help get me to that destination. I found out later that the missionary couple in Yantai had been praying earnestly that I would arrive safely. Little did they know that their prayers helped to send my angel to sit right beside me on a crowded airplane.

Does Jesus mean "anywhere" for you as well?

Often in our lives we do something and then wonder why we did what we did. I remember those thoughts I had on the plane that day. "I hope that nobody sits beside me so that I can get some rest." After this happened, I could not help but think about Hebrews 13:2 which says, ***"Be not forgetful to entertain strangers: for thereby some have entertained angels unawares."*** I had wanted to get some rest and did not want anybody to sit in the seat next to me. Yet the Lord in His mercy sent an angel to help me get to my destination. I am happy that this was one time the Lord did not allow my wishes for rest to overpower His divine protection. My friend, no matter where you are today, remember that our angels are around us all the time. Whenever we are in need, they are always there and ready to help, whether or not we know it. Praise God for our guardian angels!

CHAPTER 23

Jesus Loves YOU!!

(Yantai, Shandong Province, China)

For whatever reason, sharing the gospel was more open in the northern part of China than in the southern part. So, when I moved from Sichuan (in the south) to Shandong (in the north), I was so amazed at the difference. I didn't have to worry about being watched for everything I said, wondering if I would be kicked out of the country for saying too much about the Lord. Although I knew it was still against the law, it appeared that the people were more open to hearing it.

While living in the northern part of China in Shandong Province, I taught a seventh-grade English class. Most of these seventh graders loved English, so it was a lot of fun having conversations with them. One day I decided that I would take the English/Chinese Bibles I had and invite some of my students to my home to practice their English. I strategically placed the Bibles on my coffee table, hoping and praying that someone would pick one up. Sure enough, one student fell for my plan, and as we were sitting around the table, he picked up the Bible and started leafing through it. Without thinking twice, I asked him if he would like to have it. He was so delighted and said, "Oh good, I can practice my English." After the students left that evening, I knelt and prayed that the Holy Spirit would begin His work in the life of that child. About three weeks later I received an invitation to dinner from the parent of this particular child. I was scared to death, because I knew that I could be in some serious trouble if the parent of this minor child knew I had given the child a forbidden Bible. Naturally, I did some serious praying that day.

When I first met the father, I didn't quite know what to expect, so I was pleasantly surprised when he said in perfect English, "I just want to personally thank you for giving my son that Bible. When my son brought it home that night and shared it with me, I began to read it, and I felt such peace." Talk about relief!! Naturally, I was praising the Lord in my spirit for the rest of the evening. The father was a business man, so he had invited some of his friends to meet me, his son's foreign English teacher. Chinese people love to sing and during the meal, the father asked me to sing an English song. I was stunned because I really can't sing, but reluctantly I replied, "Wait a minute, let me think of a good song." About that time, the son said, "Why don't you sing the song you taught us last week at your house?" So, for the next few minutes, I sang *"Jesus loves me this I know..."* to a group of Chinese businessmen. The young boy started singing about the love of Jesus with me. After singing, everybody started talking again, and although I couldn't understand everything they said in their Chinese language, I knew that they were talking about Jesus. Later that evening, in the quietness of my own home, I couldn't help but praise the Lord for this eventful and precious evening.

Does Jesus mean "anywhere" for you as well?

This is a time when I must admit that I did the exact opposite of what the Bible says, but yet, in His mercy, even though I was letting my fear for the situation overwhelm me, He still worked it out for His glory. I relate this to you because Mark 13:11 says, ***"But when they shall lead you, and deliver you up, take no thought beforehand what ye shall speak, neither do ye premeditate: but whatsoever shall be given you in that hour, that speak ye: for it is not ye that speak, but the Holy Ghost"***. Here I was so worried about what I would say when I met the student's father because I thought he would be upset when he found that I had given his son the Bible. To the contrary, the father wanted to thank me. God is so good!

> *I almost missed a chance to talk about Jesus, but He didn't let me.*

I almost missed a chance to talk about Jesus, but He didn't let me. Not only did He give me the opportunity to talk about Him, but I was also able to sing about His love for them. What an awesome God we serve. Take it from me, wherever you are my friend, don't worry about saying the right thing to others about Jesus, because it won't be you speaking anyway: I know that what I said that night wasn't me speaking, but the Holy Spirit was speaking through me. God's word says it, and this experience proves to me that His Word is true.

CHAPTER 24

Chinese Mud Pit

(Road to Chengdu, China)

If you have travelled to China, you know that most of the roads there are not easily navigated because many are unpaved. For Laurie and me, our time at the university was over, and we would be heading back to the United States. In order to get there, we had to first ride in a car for 180 miles to the nearest train station, then travel by train, before eventually catching a plane to Hong Kong. We knew that the car trip would be long, so we had planned to leave at six in the morning so that we could do some shopping that afternoon in Chengdu, the capital of Sichuan. We figured that we could shop most of the afternoon, and then get a good night's rest, before catching the train the next day.

Halfway through our car ride, we ran into a traffic jam that would last nearly five hours. Not only was there a traffic jam, but the rain came down in torrents. The dirt roads on which we were travelling became one huge mud pit. What seemed like thousands of cars were stuck in the mud, and I knew that no one was going anywhere anytime soon. Since the cars had all bottlenecked and it was raining, the mud only got thicker and thicker. It seemed that hundreds of cars were struggling to get out of the pit at the same time. Several times we exited the car for a few minutes, but it was like stepping into a giant pile of muddy quicksand. I must admit this was one time that I wished I were anywhere except there. We sat there for hours listening to horns honk and Chinese people losing their tempers.

We were travelling with several Chinese people, and although the friends who accompanied us were not Christians, one of them asked that we pray to get out of the mud pit. I prayed, and although my prayer was not answered immediately, indeed it was answered. The rain stopped eventually, and we were on our way. We arrived late in the evening, and although we missed out on our afternoon shopping in the big city we were just happy to be out of the giant pit of mud.

Does Jesus mean "anywhere" for you as well?

Once again, I learned a valuable lesson—that prayer should be our first option when we are in trouble. I regret that it was a non-Christian Chinese person who had to teach me that lesson by asking me to pray—I should have already been praying from the moment I knew we had a need! Psalm 105:4, 5 reminds me to, *"Seek the LORD, and his strength: seek his face evermore. Remember his marvelous works that he hath done; his wonders, and the judgments of his mouth."* Today, my friend, wherever you are, remember to seek the Lord first and then look back and remember the marvelous works He has done in your life.

CHAPTER 25

Monkeys on Emeishan

(Mt. Emeishan, Sichuan, China)

As a child my favorite animals in the zoo were the monkeys. One question had always bothered me, however. Why did they have to be caged? Even as an adult I dreamed of what it would be like to see monkeys in the wild—and soon I would have the privilege of finding out.

During our stay in China, Laurie and I decided to travel during our summer break. Initially we were undecided as to where to go. We used one of our tourist books and began to search for a place in China that appealed to us. As my friend researched some of the places to which we might travel, she came across a famous mountain called Mt. Emeishan. As she read, I was impressed with the book's mention that visitors might see wild monkeys as they walked along the mountain trail. The book related that the monkeys could be quite dangerous because often they would bite, steal from, or scare foreigners. At that time, I did not care because I only wanted to see a monkey in the wild. After much discussion, we decided that this was the place we wanted to visit for the next two weeks.

Thankfully the Lord supplied a Chinese student who would accompany us. Laurie spoke Chinese fluently, however, having a native Chinese speaker travel with us was an added blessing. When we arrived at the starting point for the trek up the mountain, we hired a local Chinese tour guide to carry our luggage. Our first day of climbing the mountain was incredible, but by the end of the day I was disappointed that we had still not seen any monkeys. Late in the afternoon of the second day, as we were hiking up the mountain, some foreigners from Germany were coming down. They said to be careful, that there were wild monkeys further up, and that the monkeys had bitten them. They showed us the teeth marks on their arms, and I began to have second thoughts about wanting to see these creatures. However, we had come this far and decided to move on.

A few minutes later, the monkeys began to come out of the trees. I counted five of them—four babies and what appeared to be the mother. My first reaction was to run because the largest of the monkeys did not look very happy as she scurried out of the tree. After running a few hundred yards away, I stopped to turn around and realized that my poor friend was surrounded by the four baby monkeys, and the mother was not too far behind. The Chinese student who was with us yelled to my friend to drop the bag that she was carrying. She slung it down the mountain and mother and babies chased after it. I know those monkeys had to be disappointed because the only contents of the bag were candy, water, and a roll of toilet paper.

Does Jesus mean "anywhere" for you as well?

As I contemplate this experience I can't help but be reminded of Psalm 84:11, which says, *"For the LORD God is a sun and shield: the LORD will give grace and glory: no good thing will he withhold from them that walk uprightly."* So today, my friend, if you are asking for something, and the Lord does not appear to be answering, could it be that the good thing you are asking for isn't that good after all? For me, it took five monkeys on a Chinese mountain to help me understand that the Lord really does not withhold any good thing from His children. What I had thought would be a good thing, in the end, actually was not!

CHAPTER 26

"Karen, It's Time to Get Up!"

(Hotel somewhere in China)

This is one of those experiences that would forever change the way I looked at my devotion time with the Lord. It happened in a small hotel room in China. I cannot remember the circumstances exactly, but I do remember the experience. I had been traveling alone in China and had gotten a hotel room for the night, before having to catch an early morning flight the next day. Prior to this experience, each morning I had attempted to set aside at least an hour for prayer and Bible study. I went to bed that night knowing that I needed to rise very early the next morning in order to be at the airport on time. If I wanted to spend that hour with the Lord, I had to awaken at three o'clock so that I could arrive at the airport by five. That night I specifically asked the Lord that if that hour with Him was important to Him, that He would have to awaken me at three, instead of four—the time that I would set my alarm. After my prayer, I set my alarm for four o'clock, knowing that I wouldn't have that hour with Him if I woke up at that time, but knew the Lord would understand my busy schedule for that day, and would understand if I didn't spend that hour with Him—just that one time.

For those of you who have heard the Lord's voice speak to you, you will know what I am saying, because out of a deep, deep sleep, I actually

> *That night I specifically asked the Lord that if that hour with Him was important to Him, that He would have to awaken me.*

heard an audible voice call my name and say, "Karen, it's time to get up." I woke with a start to find I was all alone in the room, but immediately looked at the clock, and sure enough, it said 3:00. From that moment on, I realized something very important: all of my life I had thought I was doing the Lord a favor by taking the time out of my day to spend with Him. The reality, however, was starkly different: I had always been selfish with my time with Him, because those thoughts were only about what God could do for me at that time. I had never really thought about our relationship as being two-sided. It was always about ME, and what the Lord could do for ME. After this experience I realized that God loved me so much that He would actually take the time to wake me up, by calling out my name, at such an odd hour. My alone time with Him was so important to Him, that He wasn't about to wait to let that alarm clock awaken me that day. I remember thinking how wonderful it was to have the Creator of the universe take the time to literally call my name, and let me know I had an appointment with Him.

Does Jesus mean "anywhere" for you as well?

Isaiah 50:4 says it all. *"The Lord GOD hath given me the tongue of the learned, that I should know how to speak a word in season to him that is weary: he wakeneth morning by morning, he wakeneth mine ear to hear as the learned."* Friend, wherever you are today, remember that it is He that woke you up this morning. You may have an alarm clock, but it only can make noise. The Creator of the universe is the One who allows you the ear to hear that noise and the breath to live that day. My friend, do not be as I was and have a one-sided relationship with the Lord. It is not just about you and what you can get from Him! It is really about what you can give Him—your love and your time. I love the time I can spend with Him, but after this experience in that hotel room, I realized that He, too, loves that time with me. It's not just about what I can get from Him, but what I can give him as well. All relationships take time, but if the God of the universe could waken me at three in the morning because He valued that time with me, the God of the universe also wants to spend daily time with you as well.

CHAPTER 27

2 A.M. Taxi Ride

(Somewhere in China)

Why do we so often in life do crazy things without thinking about the consequences, but then later on we have to ask ourselves, "What in the world was I thinking?" Well, this is one of those times. Laurie and I were—again—traveling by train in China. This particular time the train arrived in the town where we were going at two o'clock in the morning. We departed the train station without knowing exactly where we were going to go. We hailed a taxi, and my friend asked the driver in Chinese to take us to a hotel. He drove us around for a while, and we were beginning to think that what we had heard from other foreigners was true. Several foreigners that we had met had told us that many Chinese people like to charge foreigners extra, because they know they are foreigners and have more money. After riding around for what felt like eternity, he took us to a nice-looking hotel, but we were turned away because we didn't have enough money to afford a room. We then asked him to take us to a cheaper hotel, which he did, but, unfortunately, they would not accommodate foreigners. After the third try, I think the taxi driver was ready for his shift to end, so within minutes we were finally at a hotel that was reasonable (if my recollection is correct, I think it was $2 for the night, compared to the $20 the first hotel wanted to charge us. I can't remember the exact cost, but I know we could finally afford it.) So, after nearly three hours of driving around looking for a room, we finally were able to rest our heads on our tiny little cots at the inexpensive hotel, and within minutes we were fast asleep. Once more the Lord in His mercy had kept us safe in the night.

Does Jesus mean "anywhere" for you as well?

When I think about how foolish we were to travel in China alone at night like this, I am reminded of the text in Psalm 92:1 and 2 that says,

"It is a good thing to give thanks unto the LORD, and to sing praises unto thy name, O most High: To shew forth thy lovingkindness in the morning, and thy faithfulness every night," The Lord had been so good to us during the day, but He was faithful to us that night as well, protecting us even when we were doing something a little bit foolish. He not only showered His lovingkindness on us as we travelled during the day, but He blessed us once again by being faithful to us, even in the dark of night. Friend, it doesn't matter what time of the day it is, God is still a loving and faithful God, no matter if it's early in the morning or 2 a.m. in a taxi in a foreign land.

CHAPTER 28

Follow Your Dreams

(Beijing, China, Great Wall)

As a young person I knew that if ever I visited a country outside of the United States, I wanted it to be China. I never dreamed, though, that I would spend eighteen months of my life there. I remember in sixth grade I looked at a picture of the Great Wall of China in one of my history books and dreamed of one day visiting this magnificent structure. I imagined myself walking on this Wonder of the World. Some twenty years later this dream became a reality because on June 29, 1994, I personally walked on the Great Wall of China. During that trip I also went to the famous Tiananmen Square and the Summer Palace.

At the time, I travelled alone so not only did my dream come true, but the Lord blessed me to be able to travel in a foreign country without knowing the language and yet managing to get around. There are some experiences in life that, when I remember them, I cannot help but KNOW that although I was physically alone, I was still protected by an unseen hand. I could not have accomplished the things I did had the LORD not been with me. I have enough trouble travelling in this country where I can read the signs, speak the language, and at least see a familiar face. When I made this trip, I had none of that. I was unable to read Chinese; therefore, I could not read the signs. I could not speak the Chinese language; therefore, I could not ask for help. Even the people around me looked different than I did.

No one can tell me that I travelled alone because I know my friend Jesus was beside me during the entire journey. I never saw Him, but had He not gone with me, I could not have accomplished my mission. Praise the LORD, because none of us are ever really alone, because He is there, even if we may not even know it.

Does Jesus mean "anywhere" for you as well?

Regardless of who you are, I believe that all of us are called of the Lord to have a "dream" for our lives. When I look back at the experience of standing on the Great Wall of China and actually trekking up this magnificent structure, I get goosebumps. I realized that some twenty years earlier the Lord had placed this dream in my heart and that with His help, it actually became a reality. As I mentioned earlier, never in my wildest dreams would I have thought I would live in China. My challenge for you today, wherever you are, whatever you are doing, is to advise you to dream, and dream big! Do not worry when your dream does not come true right away because for me twenty years was a long wait. Be sure to include God in your dreams, and as time moves along, I believe that you will see your dreams become a reality. Ephesians 3:20 tells us, *"Now unto him that is able to do exceeding abundantly above all that we ask or think, according to the power that worketh in us."* Although I had dreamed about one day standing on this Great Wall, I knew God had done for me abundantly more than I had originally asked. Praise God for those dreams He puts in our hearts. Today, dream and dream big; then watch Him do much more than you could even begin to imagine.

Chapter 29

The Lost Suitcase

(Began in Hong Kong—Ended in Collegedale, Tennessee)

A week before leaving Yantai, China, I had stomach discomfort, and I remember sitting balled up in pain in a corner of my apartment. The pain lasted almost twenty-four hours, and I was so glad when it finally subsided.

The night before I was leaving Mainland China for Hong Kong, my stomach pain came back. I prayed as I never had before, asking the Lord to please allow me to get to Hong Kong because I knew that a Seventh-day Adventist Hospital was located there and I was hopeful that the staff could speak better English than in mainland China and that they would be able to help me. About twenty minutes later the pain left and I had a great night's rest. The next morning, I arrived in Hong Kong. Later that afternoon I was so surprised when I met up with a college professor from Southern, the university I had attended in Tennessee. He and his wife had been doing missionary work in mainland China for the summer, and they just happened to be in Hong Kong at the same time I was. He introduced me to his wife, and I remembered that I had gone to grade school with their daughter.

That Saturday night we attended a church-sponsored event, and my stomach pain returned. I asked my friend if she would take me to the hospital a few doors down from where we were staying. After running a few tests, the doctors discovered that I needed gall bladder surgery, and it had to be done right away. Now, I was supposed to fly back to the United States in a few days, so after getting the news about the surgery I called my mom and told her that I would not be coming home any time soon. I asked her if she could come be with me, but because my dad was ill, she decided to ask my aunt, her sister, who had just retired, to come instead. Of course, it would take her a few days to get there, so I would have to have my surgery without any family around, but the Lord had another option to comfort me. The professor and his wife were right by my side the entire time of my surgery. In fact, she called my mother often to give her updates.

A few days after my surgery, I was lying in the bed wondering where my aunt and I would stay once I got out of the hospital. A few minutes later a nurse, whom I did not recall having seen before, came in and began a conversation with me. I was surprised to find out that she was the Director of Nurses at the hospital and had heard the story of my being a missionary leaving China, heading to the States, and ending up in the hospital. After a few minutes of conversation, she asked me where I would stay after I got out. I told her I did not know but that I had an aunt who was on her way to be with me, and we would probably have to find a hotel. She said, "I have a big house. Why don't you and your aunt come stay with me while you recuperate?" Of course I did not object! After she left my room, I began to praise the Lord for answering my prayer so quickly. The day I left the hospital, my aunt from Tennessee arrived and we moved in with the Director of Nursing for the next few weeks.

> *I began to praise the Lord for answering my prayer so quickly.*

After my recuperation, it was time to return to the States. I did have one more dilemma though, and that was that my doctor told me not to lift more than five pounds for at least six weeks. I knew this would be impossible, because my flight home was at a totally different time than my aunt's. She would leave a day earlier than me. That meant that I would have to travel alone with my two seventy-pound suitcases, which I had since I had spent a whole year in China, and everything I owned was in those two suitcases. I also knew that I would have at least five different layovers that would require me to pick up my suitcases at the different airports. My aunt and I prayed about the situation. The next day I took her to the airport and then returned to prepare for my trip home. When I arrived at the airport the next day a missionary in Hong Kong helped me check in my luggage at the baggage terminal. As I was purchasing my ticket, I explained the situation to the stewardess who suggested I check in my carry-on luggage also if I wanted. I boarded that plane with just my purse on my shoulder.

At my first stop, Seoul, South Korea, I went to the luggage belt wondering who in the crowd I might ask to help me lift my suitcases. After almost twenty minutes, I stood there noticing that my bags had not appeared on the belt and realized that I was standing at the terminal alone. Everyone else had picked up their bags. I went to the terminal and told the man behind the counter that my bags never came. He checked his computer and got a terrible look on his face. "Ma'am," he said, "I am sorry, but your luggage got on the wrong plane; it was put on the plane behind you. We will have it delivered to your house in Tennessee." I am sure the man behind the counter thought I was crazy because I remember saying, "Praise the Lord, it really is ok." I left that baggage terminal, purse in hand, praising the Lord once again for answering my prayer. Somewhere along the flight I can remember another passenger looking at me and saying, "Ma'am, you sure do travel light," and I had to chuckle to myself thinking, "If he only knew!" I stopped at five different airports, never once having to go to the baggage counter.

After my mom and dad picked me up in Atlanta, I asked them to stop at a store to buy clean clothes that I could wear until my luggage arrived. To my utter amazement, the very next day, there was a knock on my front door, and standing in front of me was a man delivering my two seventy-pound suitcases. He too must have thought I was nuts because I gave him the biggest hug and thanked him profusely for being an answer to my prayer. Never once did I ever dream that losing luggage could be such a blessing.

Does Jesus mean "anywhere" for you as well?

Isaiah 55:8, 9 sums up this experience for me very well. *"For my thoughts are not your thoughts, neither are your ways my ways, saith the LORD. For as the heavens are higher than the earth, so are my ways higher than your ways, and my thoughts than your thoughts."* I can remember standing at the baggage terminal in South Korea waiting for my luggage and wondering who in the crowd I could ask to assist me with it. I never dreamed that He had a different plan that was so much better than I could have imagined. Even as I write this morning, I know without a shadow of a doubt that He has even better plans for me today. I encourage you, wherever you are today, to know that although we try to make our own plans, His ways are so much better.

Chapter 30

Tears at the Airport

(Airport in Kiev, Ukraine)

The day that I finalized my plans to go to the Ukraine to teach English at an English language school, I was assured that someone from the school would be there to pick me up. I felt a little uneasy about this, and it wasn't helped along by the fact that, because of my quick decision to go to the Ukraine, I had not had time to get a visa. Again, I was reassured that we could work on this once I got to the country. I had my reservations about this, but decided to step out in faith and go despite the fact that I didn't know exactly who I would be meeting, and that I would be travelling without a visa to get into the country.

When I got off the plane and went into the airport I was puzzled as to which line to get into as all of them were so long and I couldn't read any of the signs because not one of them was in English. After about a twenty-minute wait in line, I stepped up to the booth where the attendant said, "No visa," and I attempted to explain to him that the people with my visa document was outside waiting for me. He then told me to go to the visa booth and fill out some papers. This man could not speak English, so he sent me to another place and there I was, back at the end of a long line, again. I kept going back and forth, from one place to another, becoming more and more frustrated each time. I kept doing this for what seemed like hours.

After about the fourth time I went to a corner to pray about the situation, but, instead of praying, I began to cry. The first tear was about to fall when a lady who spoke English approached me and asked me if she could help. I explained to her my situation, and she talked to one of the Ukrainian guards. She explained my problem to him, but he said that without a visa I could not leave. I looked up, and at that moment I saw a man holding a sign with my name written on it. Somehow the man that was supposed to pick me up had gotten through customs on the other end of the airport. After standing in line again, with the help of my new friend, I was finally authorized to leave.

Does Jesus mean "anywhere" for you as well?

Joshua 1:5 is one of my favorite texts, and after this particular experience in life, I found out the power of its truthfulness. It reads as follows, *"There shall not any man be able to stand before thee all the days of thy life: as I was with Moses, so I will be with thee: I will not fail thee, nor forsake thee."* Many times in life I have found myself knowing something in my head, but at the same time trying to truly believe what I know to be true. I must admit I knew that the Lord promises never to leave or forsake me, but standing, in that airport all alone, was one of those times when I really began to doubt whether this was true. However, as always, He appears at just the right time. When I was on the edge of tears, He sent the English-speaking lady and the man holding the sign with my name on it. Each day of our lives, we encounter experiences we may not understand, but as always, His words about never forsaking us are so true. My friend, today, wherever you are, if you need to claim Joshua 1:5, please do. I can attest from every experience I have shared with you that I know for certain He does not fail, and He will not forsake you. You can always take Him at His Word.

CHAPTER 31

A Break In-Between

(Began in Kiev, Ukraine—Ended in Zigong, Sichuan, China)

There are times in our life when the Lord does things, and we wonder later why they happened that way. This is one of those experiences that took place in my life. I had spent a year in Sichuan, China, and after that year, I returned to the states for a few short months. During that time, my sense was that of the Lord calling me to the Ukraine. After making the proper arrangements, I went to the Ukraine with the intention of staying a whole year and teaching at one of their English language schools. Other than the part of the story where no one was there to pick me up at the airport when I arrived, everything else went well for the first few weeks.

A few short weeks into my stay, I noticed a strange knot on my foot, and at the same time my feet were beginning to itch unbearably. I had no idea what caused this, and I called a Ukrainian doctor who subsequently treated me at my house one night. He was unable to diagnose my problem, and the next day I went to my school director. After having looked at my foot, his words convinced me to go and get medical treatment. He said, "Looks like leprosy to me." Naturally that frightened me, and after much prayer, I decided that it was best I return to the United States. When I arrived, the doctor I saw had no idea what it was, and suggested that it was stress related and sent me back home. I never knew the cause, but praise the Lord, after a few days it disappeared on its own. But now I was in a dilemma as to what to do next. Of course, I did some fasting and praying about which direction to go with my life, when a month or so later, I received a letter from the university I had recently left in China. My Foreign Affairs Officer in Sichuan requested that I return. This time it was not the church that made the request—it was the Chinese government. What an honor this was for me! I assumed I had done a good job when I was there before, and they had decided to invite me back. Within a few short weeks, I was back in Sichuan, China, for a second year.

Does Jesus mean "anywhere" for you as well?

When I think back on this experience I often wonder why I went to the Ukraine only to have to leave after a few short weeks. This happened in the middle of my term, and yet I ended up right where I started—back in China. I guess it was just one of those breaks that I will never truly understand. The only thing I can think of is that the Lord was not finished with me yet in China. I also think of the text in Philippians 1:6 that says, ***"Being confident of this very thing, that he which hath begun a good work in you will perform it until the day of Jesus Christ."*** He still had work for me to do in China, not in the Ukraine. I only hope and pray that my break between helped somebody, and my trip was not wasted. My friend, wherever you are today, you may be in a break in your life, but as the text says, He which started the work in you will perform it until Jesus comes. One day, when I get to heaven, I hope to ask the Lord what the purpose of my Ukrain experience was about, but until then, I will just know that life is a journey, and that there are times on this earth that we may never know the reason for certain things.

Chapter 32

Resurrection

(Yantai, China, Shandong Province)

Having traveled so much in my lifetime, I have met many people. This chapter is about one lady in particular who will always stand out in my memory. Many of the Chinese people I met had English names because they knew that most foreigners wouldn't remember their Chinese names. When I arrived in Yantai, in Shandong Province, one of the first older ladies I met introduced herself as "Resurrection." I thought that this was such an awesome name, and after hearing her personal testimony I knew why she called herself that. One day she told me her story.

As a younger woman, she had spent several years in a Chinese prison for being a Christian. She loved to sing, and she would often sing while she was sitting in her jail cell. In fact, she said she sang nearly every day. One day, as she was singing, the jailer yelled at her and told her to stop singing, but she refused. She kept on singing until one day when the jailer opened the cell door and told her to leave because he was sick and tired of listening to her sing! Her songs of praise helped her to once again be resurrected to a life of freedom.

Sometime later, I asked her what her favorite song was, and she said, "I Know Who Holds Tomorrow," by Ira Stanphill. At the time I had never even heard of this song, so one day she taught it to me, and from then on, whenever we would get together we would sing it. Naturally, this song is now very sentimental to me.

Other than teaching me a wonderful new song, Resurrection also taught me another very important lesson. I hadn't been in Yantai a very long time when I asked Resurrection if she would like to have Bible studies with me. She was thrilled, so from then on, we would get together as often as we could, and sing and then study together. One evening as we were studying a lesson on health, I made a statement telling her that it might be difficult for her to give up some of her bad eating habits, but that with God's help, she could do it. She looked at me and said, "IF God said it, then I will do it." We finished our study, and after she left I really wondered if she meant what she had just said. A few days later I would find out that she really did mean it.

The next week Resurrection and I were invited to dinner at a Chinese restaurant with some of our other Chinese friends. In front of us that night were all kinds of unclean foods, but to my utter amazement, Resurrection refused every single thing that the Bible had told her a few days ago that was unclean. She refused to eat any of it! At the end of the meal, I asked her if passing up that food was difficult, and she said with boldness, "IF God said not to eat it, then I won't." That night, she proved to me that she was right.

Does Jesus mean "anywhere" for you as well?

For those of you who may be like me and never have heard the song, "I Know Who Holds Tomorrow" by Ira Stanphill, I suggest that you look at all the words one day, and think about your own life. I think the chorus is so beautiful because it says, "I know who holds tomorrow, and I know who holds my hand." So my friend, where ever you are today, please remember WHO holds your tomorrow, and when you do, then you will also know that HE is the one that will hold your hand, as well. Not only will He hold your hand, but in Isaiah 49:16 it says, *"Behold, I have graven thee upon the palms of my hands; thy walls are continually before me."* Think about this for a moment. Not only does He hold our hand every day, but He also has our names written on the palms of His hands. So today, no matter what problems you may be facing, remember His hands have got you covered.

Chapter 33

Chinese Kindergarteners

(Yantai, China, Shandong Province)

Every one of us loves to feel loved, and this is one of those times that I felt much love through someone else's tears. This situation was due to a group of six- and seven-year-old Chinese kindergarteners. I had been teaching a group of kindergarten children for almost five months. I had always felt they loved me, but I never really knew how much until the day I left China.

I was to leave Yantai at nine o'clock in the evening. At noon that day all eight of my Chinese kindergarteners showed up at my apartment and began to cry. Naturally, I started to cry also. One little boy cried so much that he began to throw up all over my floor. Then a Chinese kindergarten teacher came over and began to clean the floor, and she also began to cry. We all sat there crying for what seemed like an eternity. Another little boy cried so hard that he broke out in hives. Two o'clock was naptime for the children, and at that point they finally had to leave. It really was terrible, and I remembered that all these tears were shed because of me.

I know my friends and family love me, but the day that eight small children cried their hearts out because I was leaving made me long for that day when Revelation 21:4 becomes a reality. No more tears! One day, my friend, you and I will never be separated from those we love ever again.

Does Jesus mean "anywhere" for you as well?

Revelation 21:4 says, *"And God shall wipe away all tears from their eyes; and there shall be no more death, neither sorrow, nor crying, neither shall there be any more pain: for the former things are passed away."* Praise the Lord for this text. My friend, today, wherever you are, whatever you are doing, please know that one day this text will be a reality, and ALL your tears will be gone. One day, and I believe real soon, ALL tears of sadness will be gone, vanished, never to reappear again. Tears of death, tears of separation, tears of pain, tears of loneliness, will one day be no more. Today, praise the Lord for His assurance of no more sorrow of any kind. For those of you I've met on my life's journey, and we are now separated by distance, please remain faithful to our Lord and Saviour, so that when, by God's grace we make it to heaven, I can look for you, and be reunited with you, never to part again. I truly do long for that day of reunions—what a wonderful day that will be!

CHAPTER 34

Way of Escape Already Planned

(Began in McAllen, Texas — Ended in Guatemala City, Guatemala)

I had been teaching in McAllen, Texas, one year and it was one week before our summer vacation. I had planned to work at an orphanage in Guatemala over the summer, so just like the students, I was anxious for the school year to be over. About a week before school ended, my students and I were talking about our summer plans. When I told them my plans, one student got really excited and informed me that she had an aunt and uncle who lived in Guatemala City and that she would get their phone number to pass on to me before I left so that I could visit them while I was there. I remember thinking to myself that I was sure I would have no time to visit her relatives, so I just brushed it off.

The school year ended, and I went to Tennessee to spend a few days with my mom and dad before leaving for Guatemala City. The night before I was to leave I received a phone call from this particular student's mother wanting to make sure I had her sister's phone number in Guatemala. She said, "If you need anything, you can just call her, and she will be more than happy to help you." I thought that was really kind, so I wrote down the number without a clue as to how important that phone number would turn out to be.

The next morning, I boarded the plane headed for Guatemala City and was told that someone would meet me at the airport when I arrived. It was about eleven o'clock in the morning when we finally landed. After getting off the plane, and grabbing my luggage, I began to search for anybody who might have come to pick me up. An hour or so passed and I began to panic— everybody started leaving the airport, and I realized that I was standing there all alone. I knew that I was in trouble. It was a Sunday, and I knew that I couldn't call anybody in the offices in the United States because they would all be closed over the weekend. I prayed about what to do and it dawned on me that I still had the phone number of my student's aunt. This was my only option. I located someone in the airport who gave me coins to use for the pay phone. I dialed the number, and to my dismay, the lady on the other end could not speak any English, so she hung up. I had one coin left, and so I tried again. This time I got another lady who could speak English, and after explaining my situation she told me that she and her dad would pick me up within a few minutes. About fifteen minutes later, I was in the company of complete strangers, heading toward their home. When I got to their home I could not believe how modern it was and how very different from the homes I had seen on the way. This man was a high dignitary in Guatemala City, and for the next three days I was treated like a queen. I even had a maid who waited on me hand-and-foot. I could hardly believe it!

The next morning, I called the office of the General Conference in Washington, DC, who explained that their office had been given my arrival date as the following Sunday. They eventually contacted the orphanage where I was to work, and informed them that I was already there. So, after three days of living like a queen with total strangers, someone from the orphanage in Guatemala City picked me up. Later that evening I could not help but praise the Lord for that little girl back in Texas who insisted that I take her aunt's phone number. God had a plan even before I knew I would be in trouble.

> **God had a plan even before I knew I would be in trouble.**

Does Jesus mean "anywhere" for you as well?

Isaiah 46:10 reminds us, that *"Declaring the end from the beginning, and from ancient times the things that are not yet done, saying, My counsel shall stand, and I will do all my pleasure."* I am so amazed when I think that God already knows what is going to happen tomorrow. Regarding this situation, He knew in advance I would need that phone number, yet I almost refused to take it. I praise God for my student's persistence that I had her aunt's number. God is so good, and this experience encourages me to thank Him for knowing what is in my future. I know from experience that worrying will not change anything because what will be, will be, whether or not I worry about it. My friend, whatever situation you find yourself in this day, remember that the God of the universe knows what will happen tomorrow and even the next moment. So why not let Him plan your future instead of trying to figure it out for yourself? I am speaking to myself here when I say to listen to His leadings in life, and watch Him protect you even before you need His protection. Thank you, Jesus, for your protection, even before I need it. I guarantee it: He has a plan already for ALL of tomorrow's troubles.

Chapter 35

Night with the Bad Girls

(Jungle Streets of Guatemala)

(***Just a note: This is a continuation of the previous story)

When I first arrived in Guatemala City, I visited an orphanage there, and I was so amazed at how many little children there were in this one facility whose parents were no longer alive. Many small children came up to me, grabbed my legs, and would not let go. It was sad to see how much love these little children craved—and needed. Since someone had gotten my arrival date wrong, I was to stay in Guatemala City for a few days before heading to my final destination in Petén. I believe it was on a Sunday morning when I was told that I would be catching a bus later that evening to take me to Petén. I would not be riding the bus alone, because fortunately another teacher would be traveling the six hour bus ride with me.

    I decided that since it would be night travel on a bus, my preparations should include leaving out a blanket and a pillow just in case I was able to get some sleep. Finally, around nine o'clock in the evening, somebody arrived to take us to the bus station. After a few minutes into the trip, I took out my blanket and pillow and decided to take a short nap.

    Shortly before three in the morning the bus came to a stop, and the other teacher with me informed me that it was time to get off. I thought it was a little odd because where we were dropped off was in the middle of nowhere—we were on a dirt road, and had not seen any sign of life for the past several hours. It was pitch black, and there was absolutely nothing around. We stepped off the bus, and it drove away, leaving us in utter darkness. I am so thankful that the teacher with me had a flashlight and cell phone, and he informed me in broken English that the person who was to pick us up there had overslept, and he was three hours away. This meant that for the next three hours we would have to stay where we were.

Not long after he turned out his flashlight I noticed a little activity. From out of nowhere, the ladies of the night started walking up and down the street looking for customers. This was unlike anything I had ever seen. I had had little experience with the night life, and as a naïve person, I only assumed that this kind of activity took place in big cities, never dreaming that I would be left on a dark, deserted road in the middle of nowhere with something like this taking place. I discovered that this kind of night life can take place anywhere, even on deserted roads in Guatemala!

I think I was so exhausted that the reality of the situation did not dawn on me until I arrived at my destination the next morning. At the time, I can remember being so exhausted that while we were waiting I walked a little bit off the beaten path and found a rock on which to lay my weary head for just a few minutes. My tiny blanket came in so handy that night as I lay on the dusty ground and slept for what seemed like just a few moments. Shortly around six, just as the sun was coming up, the other teacher woke me up and told me to get ready, that our ride was on the way. Within the next ten minutes there came a car speeding around the corner. We got into the car, and we arrived at our final destination, a week and three hours late. But praise God, I was finally there.

Does Jesus mean "anywhere" for you as well?

As I journey through life, I know without a shadow of a doubt that God has been with me. Had God not been with the teacher and me the night we were dropped off the bus in the pitch darkness, I probably would have been scared to death. However, as I laid my head down on that rock in the middle of the street, I could not help but think about Jacob and the night he met the Lord. I did not meet the Lord that night face-to-face as he did, but I certainly knew He was there. Proverbs 3:24 says, ***"When thou liest down, thou shalt not be afraid: yea, thou shalt lie down, and thy sleep shall be sweet."*** There is only one way that, humanly speaking, I could not have been afraid that night and it was because I knew that God was with me. Though evil was all around me, yet I was not afraid. That was because of God and His sweet peace. Friend, today, wherever you are, please be assured that you have nothing to fear this night because the Lord has promised in His Word that your sleep can be sweet and after this day, no matter what it may bring, you can lie down and not be afraid. How do I know? It is because of a time when evil was around me everywhere, yet His sweet peace kept me safe. Take it from me, you can experience that same kind of peace. Please praise God with me for these wise words written in the book of Proverbs.

Chapter 36

Giardia

(Peten, Guatemala)

Nobody likes to get sick, but being sick in a foreign country is definitely anything but fun. Even though I was only in Guatemala for a few short weeks, I somehow managed to get the dreaded sickness, giardia. Webster's Dictionary defines "giardia" as an intestinal infection caused by a giardia parasite. After I was sick with this, the locals there told me that I probably got it from drinking bad water. Apparently this was caused by the beavers who also lived in that drinking water.

With this sickness I had a high fever, chills, headache, diarrhea, and vomiting. I can remember thinking to myself that I was going to die, and I was so worried because I was the only foreigner on the campus and it was a three-hour car ride to the nearest telephone, and I figured that if I died I would probably already be dead and buried before any of my family would even know I was gone. It was a terrible feeling.

Even though I was very sick, I can remember that one night some of the local people came to my home and prayed with me, but they also tried using one of their local remedies. I might have had a high fever, and I may have been hallucinating at times, but I can still see in my memory somebody peeling potatoes, putting the potato slices on my head, and wrapping it all in a towel around my head and then pouring lemon juice over the towel. I was told to leave the towel on my head all night. I can still remember getting up, only a little while after everybody left, and removing the towel. I slept peacefully the rest of the night.

Does Jesus mean "anywhere" for you as well?

I truly believe that the Lord does give us natural remedies to use when we are sick, but this is one time when I am sure it was the prayers of all the saints who were praying for me that helped me to get over my sickness.

I am sure that many of you, too, can testify to the power of prayer. I know that, for myself, prayer is one reason I am even here to write this book. Without the prayers of the saints around the world for my safety and protection, I probably wouldn't even be here today. Even though I cannot know that specific moment when they prayed for me, I am so thankful that they did and that people everywhere are praying for our missionaries overseas. At the time when I was so sick, I was grateful for those that were surrounding me at the time with their prayers, but at so many other times, I could almost feel the prayers of friends back home—prayers of friends who were praying for me while I was off in a foreign land. Did you know that the Bible even speaks about the fact that when we do not pray for others it is a sin? 1 Samuel 12:22, 23 says, *"For the LORD will not forsake his people for his great name's sake: because it hath pleased the LORD to make you his people. Moreover as for me, God forbid that I should sin against the LORD in ceasing to pray for you: but I will teach you the good and the right way."*

Friends, where ever you are, may none of us ever forget to pray for each other. Whether we are far or near, prayers for others are so important, and I can testify to this fact. For me that night, I knew that God heard somebody else's prayer for me, and for that, I am forever grateful.

CHAPTER 37

Parrot Attack

(Jungle of Guatemala)

When I spent a summer in Guatemala, I was to work at an orphanage, located in the jungles of this country. My job would be to teach the orphan students English. One day, when I was walking to school, a huge, wild parrot appeared out of nowhere, landed on my shoulder, and began biting me. Fortunately there were students with me who began to attack him, and eventually he went away. It was then I learned about the jungle parrot that hated women, especially white foreign women. They informed me that I really needed to carry a stick with me wherever I went to protect myself from attack. I did this for a few days, and then one day I forgot.

One pre-dawn morning I woke up very early and could not go back to sleep, so I decided to walk around the campus. I thought this was a great idea because no one would be around, and I could enjoy a nice, peaceful walk. I had walked approximately one-half mile or so and happened to turn around in time to see the angry parrot flying toward me. I ducked just in time to be missed. Then I noticed the parrot sitting in a jungle tree waiting to attack again. I could see my apartment from this location, but I was quite a distance from it. I began to run, which made the bird angry, and it began chasing me again. I ducked. I did this about five times before finally arriving home safely. After taking a deep breath and thinking about the situation, I wished that I had taken my stick along with me for what I thought would be a nice peaceful walk. That morning, a huge, jungle parrot taught me an important lesson about being prepared.

> *...then I learned about the jungle parrot that hated women, especially white foreign women.*

Does Jesus mean "anywhere" for you as well?

Ephesians 6:17 says, **"And take the helmet of salvation, and the sword of the Spirit, which is the word of God:"** Whether or not you and I like it, we are in a battle of good versus evil, and in order to fight this battle, we need our spiritual weapons. The Bible tells us in this verse that our sword is His Word. When we commit His Word to memory, we are able to fight off the evil (Satan) daily. I think about that sword often and am reminded of this experience with the parrot. Had I taken my stick with me that day, that mean parrot might not have attacked me. I can relate this to taking the sword with me daily so that when that mean devil tries to attack me, I have a weapon with which to fight. It was when I forgot my stick in that jungle that this parrot really attacked because he knew I was unprepared. I myself know that when I neglect setting aside time to read and study His Word, the enemy is in place to attack. Today, wherever you are, ask yourself, "Do I have 'my sword' entrenched in my heart today?" If not, I suggest that you pick it up because it will help you to fight the enemy. It is a daily chore. Take up that sword everyday so that when the enemy approaches, you can be ready for whatever may come your way.

Chapter 38

James

(Okanogan, Washington)

Somehow in all of my travels, the Lord has financially provided for each journey. Many times He would wait until the last minute to provide exactly the right amount for a ticket, and this experience was no exception. I would never consider myself rich in the materialistic world, but somehow, the Lord provided for every trip I took.

At this particular time, I was living in Washington state in the small town of Okanogan, not too far from the Canadian border. While living there I cleaned house for a man named James who I knew was well off financially and he paid me quite well. I had also met some friends who did mission work all over the world. They had transformed a bus into living quarters and would take mission groups on different missionary endeavors. One day they approached me and asked if I wanted to accompany them on a three-week mission trip to Alaska. Of course I said yes, but when I found out the cost of the trip, I was unsure as to whether I could go. I decided to pray about it and felt impressed to raise money for my portion of the expenses. I asked several people who I knew but nobody wanted to give, so I had about given up on the idea of going when I decided to ask the man I cleaned house for. So, one day, I went to work, and told him that I wanted to go on a mission trip to Alaska. I do not even think I told him that I needed money, but the first thing he asked me was how much money I needed, and when I told him, he said, "I'll take care of it." And he did—he paid for the entire trip!

Does Jesus mean "anywhere" for you as well?

Psalms 34:10 says, *"The young lions do lack, and suffer hunger: but they that seek the LORD shall not want any good thing."* The Lord knew that I wanted to go on this mission trip, so in His mercy He allowed one person to give generously. I do not know of James' Christian walk, but never in my wildest dreams did I think that the Lord would use him to bless me so abundantly. Additionally, James was unaware of my need until I asked. My friend, wherever you are today, I hope and pray that you can take away two lessons from this experience. First, you never know whom the Lord could use to bless you, and the second lesson I learned is exactly what James 4:2 says, "Ye have not, because ye ask not." Had I not asked James, he would not have known my need, and we both could have missed our blessings. My friend, wherever you are, if you need a blessing today, remember that the Lord loves to do good things for His children. James blessed me that day, and I hope and pray that in return I was able to bless those in Alaska who the Lord allowed me to visit, because of one person's generous gift.

** Pseudonym used

Chapter 39

An Alaskan Girl

(Minto, Alaska)

While living in Okanogan, Washington, I had some dear missionary friends who took groups to places all over the world to do mission work. One year they asked if I would like to join them on a three-week mission trip to Alaska. Of course, I consented. Since the location of Okanogan, Washington, is about fifty miles south of the Canadian border, we took a bus that they had changed into a sleeping coach. We spent a week riding through Canada and then up into Alaska. When we arrived, we were to teach a one-week vacation Bible school program and return home the next week. I knew I could not pass up this opportunity.

Everything you have been told about the beauty of Canada and Alaska is true. The beauty of the scenery as we took that bus ride was spectacular! The towering mountains with snow-capped peaks, the enormous pines, and the crystal-clear blue sky made the long drive unforgettable. After finally arriving in the tiny village of Minto, Alaska, we set up our Vacation Bible School program. I remember one night a little girl really took a liking to me. One evening after our regular session I sat and talked with this little girl about the love of Jesus. I told her that Jesus loved her, and that He died to save her from her sins, and that He rose again, and that He is in heaven right now preparing a better place for her. I explained the story of salvation to her and will never forget the look on her face as I told her about the love of Jesus for her. It was so special to me, to see her reaction, because that night before our meetings I could see by her face that she was sad about something, and after sitting with her, and explaining the love that Jesus had for her, it was like I could see the countenance of her face change from sad and gloomy, to one of hope and cheer. When she left me that

> **When she left me that evening, her face said it all.**

evening, her face said it all. The love of Jesus had truly changed her, and I could see it in her eyes. Never before had I seen such a transformation in such a short time. Praise the Lord for the love of Jesus—not only for this little girl in a village in Alaska, but also for the entire world.

Does Jesus mean "anywhere" for you as well?

One day, soon and very soon, I believe that many passages of Scripture will be fulfilled, but when I think of this experience, I cannot wait until Matthew 24:31 becomes a reality. *"And he shall send his angels with a great sound of a trumpet, and they shall gather together his elect from the four winds, from one end of heaven to the other."* I believe with all of my heart that one day that trumpet will sound and angels from on high will go throughout the world to gather those of His children who have been faithful to Him. They will come from the east, from the west, from the north, and the south. I believe also that this little Alaskan girl from the remotest part of the world who accepted Jesus Christ in her life will meet her angel who will come to gather her up in his arms. What an awesome day this will be! My friend, it does not matter today where you are if you belong to Jesus and have accepted Him as your personal Savior and friend. He will send His angels to gather you up as well. One day, He is coming to get us all, and I personally cannot wait to experience that day for myself. Friend, Jesus is coming soon!!! I hope and pray that I will see you there in heaven as well.

Chapter 40

"Will That Not Be Awesome?"

(Pearisburg, Virginia)

I was a Bible worker in Pearisburg, Virginia, and had been there several months when this experience took place. What a valuable lesson I learned that day! I was studying with a Catholic man who had requested Bible studies. We had been studying for several weeks when we came to a lesson on sin and the great controversy (of good versus evil). We had begun the study when the doorbell rang, and it was the man's brother. I think he was surprised to see me there, but after a few minutes *George* told his brother that we were having a Bible study and invited his brother to join us. I was quite pleased when he said he would stay for a few minutes. After all our small talk, we resumed the study.

A few minutes later the doorbell rang again, and this time, it was George's neighbor. We chatted with the neighbor for some time and then George informed the neighbor that I was there having Bible study. Once again, George asked the neighbor to stay and join us. Sure enough, he did. Once again, I began the study. We had not gotten too far into our study this time when George's brother made a statement that I will never forget. Out of the blue he said, "Will that not be awesome when we get to heaven and it will not matter what religion we are? Here we are studying God's word, yet we all have different belief systems. George is Catholic, I am Pentecostal, *Sam* (George's neighbor) is an agnostic, and you are Seventh-day Adventist; yet all of us are in one place studying God's Word. I think it will be so awesome to be in heaven, and all of us will have the same beliefs."

I was so glad for the interruptions that day because I knew that God in His providence had impressed George's brother and neighbor to come over at just the right time. This happened not only for them to hear the word of God but to teach me an important lesson. One day all of God's children will be in the same place—heaven—sitting at Jesus' feet and believing the same message.

Does Jesus mean "anywhere" for you as well?

Many of us, myself included, often forget that heaven will not be full of people just from our own denomination. There will be people from every denomination under heaven. After this incident I was reminded that all of God's children will be there. Those who have loved Him here and obeyed His Word will be sitting at His feet, as I hope I will. Psalm 86:9 reminds me of that, for it says, *"All nations whom thou hast made shall come and worship before thee, O Lord; and shall glorify thy name."* When it says ALL nations, I believe it to mean ALL people from ALL nations will glorify His precious, holy name. Will it not be cool to be there with people from all over the world, not worrying about the church they attended here but knowing that they, too, love the same Jesus as you, and me? Today, my friend, whoever you are, wherever you are, no matter what church you go to, rejoice with me that as long as your name is written in the Lamb's Book of Life, you will one day be rejoicing with me that we finally made it. My church attendance will make no difference then because it will be all of those who love Jesus and have a daily walk with Him who will be there. Praise God that ALL nations includes ALL people. Speaking of AWESOME, that REALLY will be AWESOME!! That day will epitomize AWESOMENESS!!!

** Pseudonyms used

Chapter 41

Why Pray?

(Conyers, GA)

Several years ago, while living in Conyers, Georgia, we experienced a drought and needed rain badly. One morning while praying I asked the Lord to send rain and continued with my prayer and daily worship. After my devotion I took a walk, and I remember looking out ahead of me, seeing blue sky, and yet never once looking behind me to see the huge, ominous black cloud that was coming from the other direction.

I had been walking about ten minutes when I began to feel a sprinkle of rain. The farther I walked, the harder the rain came. At this time I finally saw the big, black cloud now on top of me, and the rain began to pour. It was then that I realized I was in trouble because I was only halfway through my normal walk. I knew I was going to be soaked, but as I walked, I began to praise the Lord for the rain, and by the time I got home, I looked like a drenched puppy.

> *The Lord brought to my attention a lesson that I should have learned earlier.*

Later that day, the Lord brought to my attention a lesson that I should have learned earlier. In the morning I had been praying for rain, yet I left my house without an umbrella. Had I been completely sincere in my praying, I should have known it would rain and be prepared by taking my umbrella. Many times in life we pray for things but are not totally sincere in our praying. I myself get so rushed in my prayers at times that I pray for things but may not really be sincere in my asking.

Does Jesus mean "anywhere" for you as well?

I love James 5:17, 18 for it says, *"Elias was a man subject to like passions as we are, and he prayed earnestly that it might not rain: and it rained not on*

the earth by the space of three years and six months. And he prayed again, and the heaven gave rain, and the earth brought forth her fruit." As we well know, without rain we would all die. Here in the Bible, Elijah prayed earnestly that it would not rain, and it did not for three- and one-half years. I do not know about you, but I would have a hard time praying for it NOT to rain for any length of time, much less three- and one-half years! During a flood or some other storm, I might pray that it stop raining, but to pray for no rain for over three years seems a long time to be without the life-giving blessing of rain. Anyway, the point is that God wants us to pray and expect Him to answer. Many times, I pray about something and expect God to answer me immediately. When this text says that Elijah prayed earnestly, I am amazed at myself in the manner that I pray. I pray for something to happen and when it does, I am amazed. Why do we not always pray expecting something to happen? I had prayed for rain that morning, but did I really expect it to rain? Evidently not, because had I thought He would have answered and it would rain, I never would have left my house without that umbrella. Had I earnestly prayed for that rain, I would have expected it to and would have taken my umbrella with me, knowing that it would rain. Friend, wherever you are at this moment, if you are praying for something, whatever it may be, expect an answer. We are told to be persistent in our prayers, but I believe that Elijah prayed earnestly expecting God to not send rain for a very long time. I believe that some prayers are not answered because we are not praying earnestly and fervently. For me that day, I prayed haphazardly, just mouthing the words without really believing He would answer. The next time you pray about anything, pray really believing He will answer, and I am sure He will.

Chapter 42

Your Anywhere

(Wherever You Are)

As a young person I never really knew what I wanted to do or be in life, and it was not until the age of forty that the Lord made it very clear in which direction He was leading me. I had just come out of a bad marriage, and I was devastated. For two years I tried my hardest to regain my self-worth, and it was during those two years that the Lord showed me that He definitely had a plan for my life, even at an older age. Through God's providence I had been living on Lookout Mountain, Georgia, while trying to decide what I was to do next. At this time I was attending a small church company located in Fort Oglethorpe, Georgia. I had not worked for nearly two years, and I knew that it was time to move on. One afternoon, I was lying in my bed resting, trying to think of where to begin looking for work when I felt that still, small voice speak to me, and ask, "If you could have any job, what would you really want to do?"

For the past two years I earnestly had been studying the Bible and had fallen in love with the Word like never before. When I heard that question in my mind, I said, "If I could have any job, I would want to teach the Bible, but Lord, You know I have to make money in order to survive, and I do not know of any place where someone pays anybody to teach the Bible." So I left it at that without realizing what the Lord's plan was. Later that day I received a phone call that would forever change my life. It was my pastor from the little church that I had been attending. He asked me if I was still looking for work and he wanted to know if I would be interested in working for him as a part time secretary. He explained that he had been selected as the Evangelism Coordinator for the Greater Chattanooga Area, and he needed secretarial help in order to prepare for a Mark Finley Revelation Seminar. I had taken some secretarial classes in college, so I knew that I could do the job. Of course, I said yes!

After I hung up the phone, I got on my knees and prayed again, this time telling the Lord that I had really wanted full-time work, but I was happy with what He had just given me. As soon as I got off my knees, the phone rang again, and it was my pastor again. He said, "Karen, I just spoke to Mark Finley who wants to know if you would be willing to give Bible studies for the other twenty work hours." I could not believe my ears! I said I would, and it was a good thing that I was by myself at the time because when I got off the phone, there was a lot of shouting and praising God in that house that day!!! For the next few months, I worked as his secretary and gave Bible studies. During the Revelation Seminar, the Lord blessed me so abundantly with several people who wanted to attend the meetings that I was able to get a small minivan, and another church member and I drove around each night with a vanload of ten-to-twenty people. Several of those dear souls were baptized at the seminar. Because of the Lord's blessing, I then became a regular Bible worker for two little churches in the area. Since that time, I have been a Bible worker in Fort Oglethorpe, Georgia, Columbia, South Carolina, Pearisburg, Virginia, Meridian, Mississippi, Conyers, Georgia, Pensacola, Florida, and (as of this writing) currently in Chatsworth, Georgia, and I have never been happier doing the Lord's work. Although I have taken some time off from the Bible work to write this book, I can honestly say that when I go out to give Bible studies to people who are looking for the truth, I know I have the best job in the world.

Does Jesus mean "anywhere" for you as well?

I have written this book with the hope that those of you that have journeyed with me for a few moments have come to the conclusion that it makes no difference where you are: The LORD is with you, wherever you go. I did not want the subject of this book to be just my overseas mission experiences but also my life's journey—wherever I happened to be at the time. It does not matter whether you are a stay-at-home mom, a mechanic in Alabama, a nurse in Texas, or a teacher in Africa, God is with you in whatever you do and wherever you go. Joshua 1:9 says, "***Have not I commanded thee? Be strong and of a good courage; be not afraid, neither be thou dismayed: for the LORD thy God is with thee whithersoever thou goest.***" May none of us ever forget that *Anywhere and Everywhere With Jesus ...* He IS WITH US.

Conclusion

Today, as I close my thoughts with you, I want to leave you with another one of my favorite passages of Scripture. It is found in Jeremiah 29:11, and I am sure many of you have read it before. It reminds us that, **"For I know the thoughts that I think toward you, saith the LORD, thoughts of peace, and not of evil, to give you an expected end."** For me, this text sums up what I hope you, dear reader, have received from the reading of this book. First of all, wherever He leads you in your life's journey, Jesus is by your side always. Not only is He near, but He also has a plan for your life, and that future plan involves eternity with Him in your heavenly home that He is preparing for you right now. Today He loves you and wants to journey with you wherever you go. If you have never accepted Him as your friend and loving Savior, here is a short prayer that you can pray as you ask Him into your life.

Dear Heavenly Father,

Thank You for Your great love for me. I know I am unworthy of that love, but because of Your Son Jesus Christ, I can have the confidence that I need to be worthy of that love. I know I have sinned and done terrible things, but because of Your Son, Jesus Christ, His righteous deeds cover all my unrighteousness. Cleanse me today with His Blood. Enter my heart, so I can begin a new life. I look forward now to this NEW journey with You, both now and always.

In Jesus' Precious Name,
Amen

Bible Studies

I believe that each one of us has a specific calling in life. I truly believe, with all of my heart, that my calling has been to lead others to Christ, often through Bible Studies. Therefore, to end this book, I have written a set of fifteen Bible studies. All you need to do is pray, read the Scripture, and write the answer. If you have trouble with a question, you can find the answer section at the end.

It is my desire that as you work through each section of these studies that the Lord will draw you closer to Him, as we all wait for His soon return. May God bless you as you continue on your own spiritual journey to our ultimate destination—Heaven.

Jesus Loves You!

1. **Read Jeremiah 31:3**

   What kind of love does the Lord have for you?

2. **Read Matthew 27:22–54**

   Does this story prove to you that Jesus loves you?

3. **Read John 3:16**

   God loved the world so much that He did what so that you and I could have everlasting life?

4. **Read John 10:11–18 (verse 11)**

   A.) What does the good shepherd do for his sheep?
   B.) Did He die because He was forced to?

5. **Read John 15:13**

   What is the greatest love?

6. **Read Romans 5:8**

   How did God show His love towards us?

7. **Read Romans 8:35–39**

   Can anything separate you from the love of God?

8. **Read 1 John 3:16**

   The love of God is known because he did what for us?

9. **Read 1 John 4:7–11**

   A.) What one word describes God?
   B.) Is it clear to you that Jesus loves you?

Eternal Life Can Be Yours!

1. **Read Genesis 15:1–6**

   How was Abram made righteous before the Lord? (verse 6)

2. Read Psalm 32:5

According to this text what three things did David do in order for the Lord to forgive his sins?

1.
2.
3.

3. Read Isaiah 45:21, 22

How many Gods are there?

4. Read Jeremiah 29:13

If we are seeking after God, will we find Him?

5. Read Matthew 7:13, 14

A.) Which gate leads to destruction?

B.) Do many or few enter in this gate?

C.) Which gate leads to life?

D.) Do many or few enter this gate?

6. Read John 3:14–16

What kind of life is promised to those that believe in Him?

7. Read John 14:6

How can you come to the Father?

8. Read John 17:3

Is knowing God important?

9. Read Acts 4:10–12

What is the only name that can save us?

10. Read Acts 16:30, 31

How can you be saved today?

11. Read Romans 3:22–24

How many people have sinned? (verse 23)

12. **Read Romans 6:23**

    A.) What is the cost of sin?

    B.) What is the gift of God?

13. **Read Ephesians 2:8–10**

    What saves us?

14. **Read Ephesians 4:7**

    Who has grace?

15. **Read 1 John 1:9**

    What happens when we confess our sins?

16. **Read 1 John 2:25**

    What has He already promised us?

17. **Read 1 John 5:11–13**

    A.) Eternal life is in His _____ (verse 11)

    B.) How can you know you have eternal life? (verse 13)

18. **Are you willing to accept the gift of salvation offered to you by a loving God, and a personal Savior? Here are the steps to help you do just that.**

    1. Accept Jesus as your personal Savior, Lord and friend.
    2. Believe that Jesus loves you, and died for your sins.
    3. Confess your sins to Him.
    4. Repent and turn away from these sins.
    5. Receive Him into your heart, and watch Him change your life.

    Is it clear to you that you can have the assurance of eternal life today?

The Signs of His Return

1. **Read Matthew 24:3–8**

    What are at least three signs that will occur before His return?

    1.

2.

3.

2. Read Matthew 24:14

What will happen right before He returns?

3. Matthew 24:23

If somebody tells us that Christ is here, should we believe it?

4. Read Matthew 24:32, 33

When we see all these signs, what should we know?

5. Read Matthew 24:36

Who is the only One who knows when He will return?

6. Read Matthew 24:44

Why should we always be ready for His return?

7. Read Matthew 25:13

Since we don't know when He is coming, what should we do?

8. Read Mark 13:35–37

If we do not watch for these signs, what could we be doing when He comes?

9. Read Luke 21:25, 26

Describe men's hearts when the powers of heaven shall be shaken?

10. Read Luke 21:28

When we see all these things begin to come to pass, what should we do and why?

11. Read Luke 21:36

What should we be doing while we watch?

12. Read 1 Thessalonians 5:1–3

When men are saying "Peace and Safety," what will then happen?

13. **Read 2 Timothy 3:1–7**

    Describe what life will be like in the last days.

14. **Read Titus 2:13**

    What is another name for the glorious appearing of our great God?

15. **Read 1 Peter 5:4**

    When the chief Shepherd appears what will we receive?

16. **Read 2 Peter 3:10**

    Describe the Day of the Lord:

17. **Read 1 John 2:28**

    What should we be doing now, so that we will not be ashamed when He comes?

18. **Read Revelation 1:7**

    Who will see Him when He comes?

19. **Read Revelation 16:15**

    He says He will come as a thief, therefore we are blessed if we do what?

20. **Read Revelation 22:12**

    When He comes what does He bring with Him?

After studying this lesson, is it clear to you that the signs mentioned in Matthew 24 and elsewhere in scripture are signs that are pointing to His soon return?

How Will Jesus Return?

1. **Read Psalm 50:3**

    When God comes will He remain silent?

2. **Read Matthew 24:27**

    What kind of light describes His coming?

3. **Read Matthew 24:29–31**

   What instrument accompanies the second coming?

4. **Read Luke 21:27**

   How will the Son of Man (Jesus) come?

5. **Read John 5:28, 29**

   The second coming of Christ will be so loud that who will hear His voice?

6. **Read John 14:1–3**

   What is the great promise He gives us in verse 3?

7. **Read Acts 1:9–11**

   How will He come?

8. **Read 1 Corinthians 15:51–58**

   When will we all be changed? (verse 52)

9. **Read 1 Thessalonians 4:15–18**

   A.) Who will rise first?

   B.) Then what happens to those who are alive?

   Where we will meet both the Lord and our resurrected friends, and loved ones?

10. **Read 2 Thessalonians 1:7–10**

    Who is coming with Jesus when He shall be revealed?

11. **Read Revelation 1:7**

    Who will see Him when He returns?

After studying this lesson, is it clear to you that one day, Jesus will come again, and take all the righteous with Him, and that this event will not be a secret, silent event?

Who Will You Obey?

1. **Read Genesis 3:1–7**

   What had God told Adam and Eve would happen if they ate or touched the fruit of the tree in the middle of the garden? (verse 3)
   What did the serpent say would happen? (verse 4)
   Who did they obey?

2. **Read Deuteronomy 11:26–28**

   This was written to the Israelites many years ago; what is God still promising you and me, if we obey the commandments of the Lord?
   What does He promise us if we obey not the commandments?

3. **Read 1 Kings 18:21**

   In this text, what question did Elijah ask the people?
   Who did he ask them to choose between?
   What was their response?

4. **Read Proverbs 16:25**

   Is it possible that we may do something that we think to be right, but discover later that that we were wrong?

5. **Read Amos 3:3**

   This text asks a question—what is that question?

6. **Read Matthew 6:24**

   Why can we not serve two masters?

7. **Read Matthew 16:24**

   If we want to follow Jesus what three things must we do?
   1.
   2.
   3.

8. **Read John 10:27**

   What do Jesus' sheep do? (Two things)

1.
2.

9. **Read John 12:35**

   Why does Jesus want us to walk in the light while we have the light?

10. **Read John 14:15**

    What will we do if we love Jesus?

11. **Read 2 Corinthians 6:2**

    When is the day of salvation?

12. **Read James 4:4**

    If we are a friend of the world then we are what to God?

13. **Read James 4:17**

    If we know to do good, and don't do it, this is called what?

14. **Read 1 John 2:3–6**

    If we say that we know God, and don't keep His commandments, what does the Bible call us?

15. **Read Revelation 21:7, 8**

    Who are those who will have their part in the lake of fire?

Is it clear to you that obedience in all things is very important to your salvation?

The Ten Commandments

Exodus 20:3–17

#1

(3) Thou shalt have no other gods before me.

#2

(4) Thou shalt not make unto thee any graven image, or any likeness of any thing that is in heaven above, or that is in the earth beneath, or that is in the water under the earth:

(5) Thou shalt not bow down thyself to them, nor serve them: for I the LORD thy God am a jealous God, visiting the iniquity of the fathers upon the children unto the third and fourth generation of them that hate me;

(6) And shewing mercy unto thousands of them that love me, and keep my commandments.

#3

(7) Thou shalt not take the name of the LORD thy God in vain; for the LORD will not hold him guiltless that taketh his name in vain.

#4

(8) Remember the sabbath day, to keep it holy.

(9) Six days shalt thou labour, and do all thy work:

(10) But the seventh day is the sabbath of the LORD thy God: in it thou shalt not do any work, thou, nor thy son, nor thy daughter, thy manservant, nor thy maidservant, nor thy cattle, nor thy stranger that is within thy gates:

(11) For in six days the LORD made heaven and earth, the sea, and all that in them is, and rested the seventh day: wherefore the LORD blessed the sabbath day, and hallowed it.

#5

(12) Honour thy father and thy mother: that thy days may be long upon the land which the LORD thy God giveth thee.

#6

(13) Thou shalt not kill.

#7

(14) Thou shalt not commit adultery.

#8

(15) Thou shalt not steal.

#9

(16) Thou shalt not bear false witness against thy neighbour.

#10

(17) Thou shalt not covet thy neighbour's house, thou shalt not covet thy neighbour's wife, nor his manservant, nor his maidservant, nor his ox, nor his ass, nor any thing that is thy neighbour's.

The Law of God

1. Read Exodus 31:18

How were the ten commandments, which were written on two tables of stone, written?

2. Read Deuteronomy 4:12, 13

How many commandments are there?

3. Read Psalm 19:7

The law of the Lord is what?

4. Read Psalm 111:7, 8

How long will His commandments stand?

5. Read Psalm 119:18

The Psalmist asked for his eyes to be opened so that he could behold what?

6. Read Psalm 119:142

God's law is what?

7. Read Psalm 119:151

How many of God's commandments are truth?

8. **Read Isaiah 42:21**

   What will the Lord do with His law?

9. **Read Malachi 3:6**

   Does the Lord change?

10. **Read Matthew 19:16–22**

    In verse 17 Jesus said that if we will enter into life, what should we do?

11. **Read John 14:15–21**

    We will keep his commandments if we what?

12. **Read Romans 3:27–31**

    Instead of making void the law through faith, what are we told to do?

13. **Read Romans 6:14, 15**

    Should we sin, because we are under grace?

14. **Read Romans 7:7**

    How do we know what sin is?

15. **Read Romans 7:12**

    What three words describe the law?

16. **Read Romans 8:3, 4**

    Is it possible for the law to be fulfilled in us?

17. **Read Romans 13:10**

    What is the fulfilling of the law?

18. **Read Galatians 2:15, 16**

    Can the works of the law save us?
    What is it that saves us?

19. **Read Galatians 3:24**

    What is the purpose of the law?

20. **Read Revelation 22:14**

    If we keep His commandments what right will we have?

    After studying this lesson is it clear to you that keeping the ten commandments does not save you, but you should want to keep them because you love Him?

The Sabbath

1. **Read Genesis 1:5**

    When does a day begin?

2. **Read Genesis 2:1–3**

    What four things did God do at creation on the seventh day?
    1.
    2.
    3.
    4.

3. **Read Exodus 20:8–11**

    A.) We are to remember what day?
    B.) What are we not to do on the seventh day?
    C.) Which day of the week is the seventh day?

4. **Read Isaiah 56:2**

    What one word describes the man who keeps the Sabbath?

5. **Read Isaiah 58:13, 14**

    What one word describes His day?

6. **Read Isaiah 66:22, 23**

    In the new earth when will all flesh come to worship the Lord?

7. **Read Ezekiel 20:12 and verse 20.**

    What is the sign between the LORD and us?

8. **Read Matthew 11:28, 29**

   If we come to Him, what does He promise for our weary souls?

9. **Read Matthew 12:12**

   Is it lawful to do well (good things) on the Sabbath?

10. **Read Luke 4:16**

    What did Jesus do on the Sabbath day?

11. **Read Luke 23:54–Luke 24:1, 2**

    A.) According to Luke 23:54, what day was Jesus crucified?
    B.) What day did the women go home and rest?
    C.) What day did the women return to the tomb and find the stone rolled away?

12. **Read Mark 16:9**

    A.) What day was Jesus resurrected?
    B.) What day is the first day of the week?

13. **Read John 19:31–33**

    The soldiers found that Jesus was already dead on what day?

14. **Read Revelation 1:10**

    A.) When was John in the Spirit?
    B.) According to these texts, Matthew 12:8 and Mark 2:27, 28, what day would be the Lord's Day?

After studying this lesson is it clear to you that the seventh day of the week, Saturday, is the Sabbath day, and are you willing to start keeping it holy?

What Does the Bible Say About Death?

1. **Read Genesis 2:7**

    A.) How did God form man?
    B.) What did He breathe into his nostrils?
    C.) After this, man became a living what?

2. **Read Genesis 2:17**

   What did God say would happen if they disobeyed by eating from the tree?

3. **Read Genesis 3:4**

   What did the serpent say would happen?

4. **Read Job 33:4**

   What gives us life?

5. **Read Psalm 115:17**

   Do the dead praise the Lord?

6. **Read Psalm 146:4**

   When we die, what happens to our thoughts?

7. **Read Ecclesiastes 9:5**

   A.) What do the living know?
   B.) What do the dead know?

8. **Read Ecclesiastes 12:7**

   A.) Where do our bodies go at death?
   B.) What about our spirit?

9. **Read Ezekiel 18:20**

   Can the soul die?

10. **Read Daniel 12:2**

    Those that sleep in the dust of the earth shall one day do what?

11. **Read Matthew 9:24**

    Jesus himself said that the little girl was not dead, but what?

12. **Read John 5:28, 29**

    A time is coming when all that are in their graves shall hear His voice and do what?

114 | *Anywhere and Everywhere with Jesus*

13. **Read John 11:11–14**

    The disciples thought that Lazarus was sleeping; instead Jesus told them plainly that Lazarus was what?

14. **Read Acts 7:59, 60**

    After Stephen asked the Lord not to lay this sin to their charge, what did he do?

15. **Read 1 Corinthians 15:22–26**

    What is the last enemy to be destroyed?

16. **Read 1 Corinthians 15:51–57**

    What is the mystery? (verse 51)

17. **Read 2 Corinthians 4:11**

    What kind of flesh do we have?

18. **Read 1 Thessalonians 4:13–17**

    A.) Who will rise first at the resurrection?
    B.) What will then happen to the righteous living?

19. **Read 1 Timothy 6:15–16**

    Who is the Only One who has immortality?

20. **Read Revelation 14:13**

    What are those that die in the Lord doing from their labors?

After studying this lesson, is it clear to you that when a person dies, his body returns to the dust of the earth, his spirit (breath) returns to God, and his soul sleeps in the grave until the second coming of Jesus?

Hell Fire

1. **Read Exodus 21:6, 1 Samuel 1:22, and Jonah 2:6**

    A.) How long would a servant serve his master? (Exodus 21:6)
    B.) Or Samuel to abide in the house of the Lord? (1 Samuel 1:22)

C.) Or Jonah in the belly of the whale? (Jonah 2:6)
D.) Are they still doing these things today?

2. **Read Job 21:30**

    The wicked are reserved for what day?

3. **Read Psalm 37:10 and 20**

    In a little while, what will happen to the wicked?

4. **Read Isaiah 65:17**

    Will we remember the bad things about this old earth?

5. **Read Jeremiah 17:27**

    Jerusalem was destroyed by a fire that could not be quenched. Is Jerusalem still burning today?

6. **Read Ezekiel 18:4 and Ezekiel 18:20**

    What happens to the soul that sins?

7. **Read Nahum 1:9**

    Will sin arise a second time?

8. **Read Malachi 4:1–3**

    Who will one day be ashes under our feet?

9. **Read Matthew 10:28**

    Who should we fear?

10. **Read Matthew 25:41**

    Who was hell fire prepared for?

11. **Read Matthew 25:46**

    Will the wicked go into everlasting punishment or everlasting punishing?

12. **Read John 3:14–16**

    What will happen to those who do not believe in Him?

116 | *Anywhere and Everywhere with Jesus*

13. Read John 5:28, 29

Where are both the righteous dead and wicked dead right now?

14. Read Hebrews 12:29

What two words describe our God?
1.
2.

15. Read 2 Peter 2:6 and Jude 1:7

A.) Why were Sodom and Gomorrah turned into ashes?
B.) Are Sodm and Gomorrah still burning today?

16. Read 2 Peter 3:7–13

A.) In verse 10 it says the earth and the works therein shall be burned
B.) What kind of heat does all of this? (Verse 10)

17. Read 1 John 5:12

If we were to burn for ever and ever in the fires of hell, we would still be alive. According to this text, if you don't have the Son, you do not have what?

18. Read Revelation 20:7–9

What does this fire do to those who try to overcome God's city and people?

After studying this lesson, is it clear to you that no one is currently burning in hell, and that when Christ descends a second time and brings judgment, that then, and only then, will hell fire begin, and that it lasts only until Satan, sin, and sinners are burned up?

What Does the Bible Say About Our Health?

1. Read Genesis 1:29, 30

What was the original diet?

2. Read Genesis 7:2, 3

- **A.)** What two classes of animals went into the ark?
- **B.)** The clean beasts went in by
- **C.)** The unclean beasts went in by

3. **Read Leviticus 11:1–12**
   - **A.)** What characteristics does a clean animal have? (verse 3)
   - **B.)** Is the pig clean or unclean?
   - **C.)** What characteristics do those clean animals have that are in the waters?
   - **D.)** Verse 12 says that those water animals that do not have and scales are what?

4. **Read Proverbs 4:17**

   Wine is associated with what "v" word?

5. **Read Proverbs 20:1**

   Wine is a_____, causing us not to be _____.

6. **Read Proverbs 23:29–32**

   Wine bites like a what? (verse 32)

7. **Read Isaiah 66:15–17**

   What will happen to those who eat swine's flesh, the abomination, and the mouse?

8. **Read Romans 12:1, 2**

   What are we to do with our bodies?

9. **Read 1 Corinthians 6:19, 20**
   - **A.)** What are our bodies referred to in verse 19?
   - **B.)** Who do our bodies belong to?

10. **Read 1 Corinthians 10:31**

    How are we to eat, drink, and act in all that we do?

11. **Read Philippians 4:13**

    Is it possible to give up some of our bad health habits?

12. Read 1 Thessalonians 5:23

What did Paul pray that would be preserved blameless unto the coming of the Lord?

13. Read 3 John 1:2

Does God want us to be in good health?

After studying this lesson, is it clear to you that your body is the temple of God, and that He desires only the best things to be put into that temple?

The Holy Spirit

1. Read Genesis 6:3–8

A.) In verse 3, God said that who would not strive with man forever?

B.) In verse 5, the Lord described the people's hearts as being what?

2. Read Psalm 51:11

What is the Psalmist's request in this verse?

3. Read Isaiah 63:7–10

Along with rebellion, what did the people do?

4. Read Matthew 12:31, 32

What is the only sin that will not be forgiven?

5. Read Mark 3:28, 29

What is the person who blasphemes the Holy Ghost in danger of?

6. Read Luke 3:21, 22

Was the Holy Ghost present at the Lord's baptism?

7. Read Luke 11:13

Will our Heavenly Father give us the gift of the Holy Spirit if we ask Him?

8. Read Luke 12:12

Who will teach us what to say when we don't know what to say?

9. **Read John 10:32, 33**

   What is blasphemy?

10. **Read John 12:35**

    Why should we walk in the new light God gives us?

11. **Read John 14:26**

    What is another name for the Holy Ghost?

12. **Read John 20:22**

    When Jesus found the disciples in the room what did He breathe on them?

13. **Read Acts 1:8**

    At Pentecost, what was the power that the Holy Ghost gave them?

14. **Read Acts 2:38**

    After we repent and are baptized what will we receive?

15. **Read Acts 4:31**

    After receiving the Holy Ghost how did they speak the word of God?

16. **Read Acts 5:32**

    God gives the Holy Ghost to those who _____ Him.

17. **Read Romans 14:17**

    A.) The kingdom of God is not about what?
    B.) What is it about?

18. **Read 1 Corinthians 2:13**

    The Holy Ghost teaches us to compare spiritual things with _____ things.

19. **Read 1 Corinthians 12:3**

    No man can say that Jesus is the Lord, except by the _____.

20. **Read Ephesians 4:30**

    We are told not to _____ the Spirit of God.

21. **Read Hebrews 3:7–15**

    In verse 8 we are told not to _____ our hearts if we hear the Holy Ghost speak to us.

After studying this lesson, is it clear to you that the Holy Spirit is important in your salvation and that the unpardonable sin is turning away from the promptings of that Spirit?

Baptism

1. **Read Matthew 3:1–6**

    Not only were the people baptized, but they also did what with their sins?

2. **Read Matthew 3:13–16**

    A.) Why was it necessary for Jesus to be baptized? (verse 15)

    B.) What kind of baptism did John perform on Jesus?

    (Was He sprinkled, immersed, or poured upon?)

3. **Read Mark 1:4–8**

    In verse 8 John said that he would baptize with water, but that Jesus would baptize with what?

4. **Read Mark 16:16**

    Is baptism important to our salvation?

5. **Read Luke 7:30**

    The Pharisees and lawyers rejected WHAT and were not baptized of him?

6. **Read Acts 1:5**

    Jesus predicted that they would be baptized with what?

7. **Read Acts 2:38**

    When we are baptized we should first do what?

8. **Read Acts 8:26–40**

   A.) In verse 36, the eunuch asked Philip a question—what was the question?

   B.) In verse 37, how did Philip answer his question?

9. **Read Acts 19:1–6**

   According to this text, would rebaptism be acceptable if a person receives new light concerning new spiritual things?

10. **Read Acts 22:16**

    What question is Jesus asking you today?

11. **Read Romans 6:3, 4**

    What spiritual significance does baptism have? (There are three things.)
    1.
    2.
    3.

After studying this lesson, is it clear to you that there is only one Biblical manner of baptism, which is by complete immersion, and that baptism is an important part of your salvation?

Tithe

1. **Read Genesis 28:20–22**

   How much did Jacob vow that he would give to the Lord if He protected him? (last part of verse 22)

2. **Read Leviticus 27:30–32**

   The tenth of our wealth shall be _____ unto the Lord.

3. **Read Deuteronomy 16:17**

   Every man shall give as he _____, according to the _____ of the Lord thy God which He hath given thee.

4. **Read Psalm 50:10**

   Who owns all the animals?

5. **Read Psalm 96:8**

   What are we to bring into His courts?

6. **Read Malachi 3:8–10**

   How have we robbed God?

7. **Read Matthew 6:25–34**

   Does God know all our needs?

8. **Read Luke 12:16–21**

   What did Jesus call this rich man?

9. **Read Luke 21:1–4**

   Which is more important to God—the amount we give or the faithfulness in which we give it?

10. **Read 1 Corinthians 9:13, 14**

    Those that preach the gospel should live of the what?

11. **Read 2 Corinthians 9:7**

    What kind of giver does God love?

12. **Read 1 Timothy 6:7**

    How much of our wealth will we take with us when we die?

After studying this lesson, is it clear to you that ten percent of your income is a holy tithe to the Lord, and the other blessings that you receive should be given as offerings to help support your local ministries within the local church?

Bible Promises

1. **Read Joshua 1:9**

   Why does the Lord tell us not to be afraid?

2. **Read Isaiah 41:10**

   What is the promise in this verse?

3. **Read Jeremiah 29:11–13**

   We must search for Him with what?

4. **Read Lamentations 3:21–26**

   What is new every morning?

5. **Read Matthew 6:25–34**

   What are we not to worry about?

6. **Read Mark 10:27**

   How much is possible with God?

7. **Read John 14:27**

   What did Jesus leave with us?

8. **Read Philippians 4:19**

   What does He promise in this verse?

9. **Read Hebrews 13:5,6**

   What is the promise that He makes to us in verse 5?

10. **Read 1 John 1:9**

    If we confess our sins, what does He promise to do?

11. **Read 1 John 2:25**

    What has He already promised us?

12. **Read Revelation 21:4**

    What does He promise to one day wipe away from our eyes?

After studying this lesson do you believe that He has promised you many great and wonderful promises and that you want to trust Him in all things?

Heaven

1. **Read Genesis 1:1**

   Is heaven a real, created place?

2. Read Isaiah 11:6

What animals are mentioned in heaven that will be kind to one another?

3. Read Isaiah 33:24

Will there be sickness in heaven?

4. Read Isaiah 35:4–10

What will happen to the eyes of the blind when the Lord comes?
What will happen to the man that is lame when the Lord comes?
What will happen to the man that cannot speak when the Lord comes?
n verse 10, what are several things mentioned that will be no more?

5. Read Isaiah 40:28–31

What will happen to those that wait on the Lord?

6. Read Isaiah 65:17

Will we remember the former things of this life?

7. Read Isaiah 65:21–24

What will we be doing in heaven?

8. Read Zechariah 8:3–5

Who will be playing in the streets of heaven?

9. Read Matthew 6:33

Instead of worrying, what is the first thing we are to be looking for?

10. Read Luke 24:39

The disciples thought that Jesus was just a spirit after He was crucified, but what kind of body did He have after His resurrection?

11. Read 1 Corinthians 2:9

Can we really comprehend what heaven will be like?

12. Read Philippians 3:20–21

He says that He will change our vile bodies into what?

13. Read Hebrews 11:16

What kind of country are our patriarchal fathers waiting for?

14. Read Revelation 21:1–27

This chapter is a beautiful description of heaven. What are a few things that get you excited about going there?

15. Read Revelation 22:1–2

Describe what the river will be like:

16. What will we be eating from?

Is it clear to you that Jesus loves you and wants to spend eternity with you in a new, heavenly home?

Answer Sheet

Jesus Loves You

1. Everlasting

2. Yes

3. He gave His only begotten Son

4. **A.)** Lay down His life **B.)** No

5. To lay down his life

6. While we were still sinners, Christ died for us

7. No

8. He laid down His life for us

9. Love

Eternal Life Can Be Yours

1. He believed in the Lord

2. Acknowledged his sin, did not hide his iniquity, confessed his transgression

3. One

4. Yes

5. **A.)** Wide **B.)** Many **C.)** Narrow **D.)** Few

6. Everlasting

7. Through His Son

8. Yes

9. Jesus

10. Believe on the Lord Jesus Christ

11. All

12. **A.)** Death **B.)** Eternal life

13. Grace through faith

14. Each one of us

15. He is faithful and just to forgive and cleanse

16. Eternal life

17. **A.)** Son **B.)** Believe in the name of the Son

The Signs of His Return

1. False Christ, deception, Wars, Rumors of wars, earthquakes, pestilences, famines

2. Gospel will be preached to the whole world

3. No

4. It is near, even at the door

5. The Father

6. He's coming at an hour we do not expect

7. Watch

8. Sleeping

9. They will fail them from fear

10. Look up, lift up your heads, for your redemption draws near

11. Pray

12. Sudden destruction

13. Perilous times, men will be lovers of self, lovers of money, boasters, proud, blasphemers, disobedient to parents, unthankful, unholy, unloving, slanderers, without self-control, brutal despisers of good, traitors, headstrong, haughty, lovers of pleasure more than lovers of God, having a form of godliness, but denying the power.

14. Blessed hope

15. Crown of life

16. Like a thief in the night

17. Abide in Him

18. Every eye

19. Watch and keep on your garment

20. A Reward

How Will Jesus Return?

1. No

2. Lightning

3. Trumpet

4. With power and great glory

5. The dead

6. He promises to come back and get us

7. In the clouds, in the same manner He left

8. At the last trumpet

9. **A.)** The dead in Christ **B.)** We will be caught up **C.)** In the air

10. The angels

11. Every eye

Who Will You Obey?

1. **A.)** They would die **B.)** They would NOT die **C.)** The Serpent (Satan)

2. **A.)** A Blessing **B.)** A Curse

3. **A.)** How long will you falter between two opinions? **B.)** God or Baal **C.)** They answered him not a word.

4. Yes

5. "Can two walk together, unless they are agreed?"

6. He will hate the one and love the other

7. Deny himself, take up his cross, and follow Jesus

8. Hear His voice, and follow Him

9. So that darkness does not overtake you

10. Keep His commandments

11. Now

12. An enemy

13. Sin

14. A Liar

15. The cowardly, unbelieving, abominable, murderers, sexually immoral, sorcerers, idolaters, and all liars

The Law of God

1. With the finger of God

2. 10

3. Perfect

4. Forever

5. Wondrous things from the law

6. Truth

7. All

8. Exalt it and make it honorable

9. No

10. Keep the commandments

11. Love Him

12. Establish the Law

13. No

14. By the Law

15. Holy, just, and good

16. Yes, but only through Jesus

17. Love

18. **A.)** No **B.)** By faith in Jesus Christ

19. It is our tutor to bring us to Christ

20. To the tree of life

The Sabbath

1. In the evening (at sunset)

2. **A.)** He ended His work **B.)** He rested **C.)** He blessed it **D.)** He Sanctified it

3. **A.)** The Sabbath **B.)** Work **C.)** Saturday

4. Blessed

5. Holy

6. From one Sabbath to another

7. The Sabbath

Answers | 131

8. Rest

9. Yes

10. He went to the synagogue

11. **A.)** Preparation Day (Friday) **B.)** Sabbath (Saturday) **C.)** First Day (Sunday)

12. **A.)** The first day of the week **B.)** Sunday

13. Preparation Day (Friday)

14. **A.)** On the Lord's Day **B.)** The Sabbath

What Does the Bible Say About Death?

1. **A.)** The dust of the ground **B.)** breath of life **C.)** soul

2. They would die

3. They would NOT die

4. The breath of the Almighty

5. No

6. They perish

7. **A.)** That they will die **B.)** Nothing

8. **A.)** Return to the earth **B.)** Returns to God

9. Yes

10. Awake

11. Sleeping

12. Come Forth

13. Dead

14. Fell asleep

15. Death

16. We shall all be changed

17. Mortal

18. **A.)** The dead in Christ **B.)** They will be caught up

19. King of Kings and Lord of Lords

20. Resting

Hell Fire

1. **A.)** Forever **B.)** Forever **C.)** Forever **D.)** No

2. Day of Judgement

3. They will be no more

4. No

5. No

6. It shall die

7. No

8. The wicked

9. Him who is able to destroy both soul and body in hell

10. The devil and his angels

11. Punishment

12. They will perish

13. In their graves

14. Consuming fire

15. **A.)** As an example to those who live ungodly **B.)** No

16. **A.)** up **B.)** Fervent

17. Life

18. Devours them

What Does the Bible Say About Our Health?

1. Every herb that yielded seed, and every tree whose fruit yielded seed.

2. **A.)** Clean and Unclean **B.)** 7's **C.)** 2's

3. **A.)** Divides the hoof, and chews the cud **B.)** Unclean **C.)** Must have fins and scales **D.)** Abomination

4. Violence

5. Mocker, wise

6. Serpent

7. They will be consumed together

8. Present them to God as a living sacrifice

9. **A.)** The Temple of the Holy Spirit **B.)** God

10. Do all to the glory of God

11. Yes

12. Spirit, soul and body

13. Yes

The Holy Spirit

1. **A.)** The Holy Spirit **B.)** evil

2. Do not take Your Holy Spirit from me

3. Grieved the Holy Spirit

4. Blasphemy against the Holy Spirit

5. Eternal condemnation

6. Yes

7. Yes

8. The Holy Spirit

9. Saying you can forgive sins

10. So that darkness doesn't overtake you

11. Comforter

12. Holy Spirit

13. The power to witness

14. The Holy Ghost

15. With boldness

16. Obey

17. **A.)** Eating and Drinking
    B.) Righteousness, peace and joy in the Holy Spirit

18. Spiritual

19. Holy Spirit

20. Grieve

21. Harden

Baptism

1. Confessed them

2. **A.)** To fulfill all righteousness **B.)** Immersed

3. Holy Spirit

4. Yes

5. The will of God

6. The Holy Spirit

7. Repent

8. **A.)** What hinders me from being baptized?
   B.) If you believe with all your heart you may

9. Yes

10. "Why are you waiting?"

11. **A.)** Death **B.)** Burial **C.)** Resurrection

Tithe

1. Tenth
2. Holy
3. Is able, blessing
4. God
5. An offering
7. In tithes and offerings
8 Yes
9. A fool
10. Faithfulness
11. The gospel
12. Cheerful
13. Nothing

Bible Promises

1. Because the Lord is with you wherever you go
2. He is with us
3. With all our heart
4. His compassions and mercies
5. What we eat, what we drink or what we wear
6. All things

7. Peace

8. He will supply all our needs

9. He will never leave us or forsake us

10. Forgive and cleanse us

11. Eternal life

12. Tears

Heaven

1. Yes

2. Wolf, lamb, leopard, goat, calf, young lion

3. No

4. **A.)** They will open **B.)** They will leap **C.)** They will sing **D.)** Sorrow and sighing

5. Renew their strength

6. No

7. Build houses, and plant vineyards

8. Children

9. Kingdom of God and His righteousness

10. Flesh and Bones

11. No

12. His glorious body

13. Heavenly

14. There is no right or wrong answer. Any answer is good.

15. **A.)** clear as crystal **B.)** the tree of life

TEACH Services, Inc.
PUBLISHING

We invite you to view the complete
selection of titles we publish at:
www.TEACHServices.com

We encourage you to write us
with your thoughts about this,
or any other book we publish at:
info@TEACHServices.com

TEACH Services' titles may be purchased in
bulk quantities for educational, fund-raising,
business, or promotional use.
bulksales@TEACHServices.com

Finally, if you are interested in seeing
your own book in print, please contact us at:
publishing@TEACHServices.com

We are happy to review your manuscript at no charge.

www.ingramcontent.com/pod-product-compliance
Lightning Source LLC
Chambersburg PA
CBHW070541170426
43200CB00011B/2508